*To Jeannie with my best*

*Raymond*

# MAMNOU'
## *— A Return To Cairo*

*By*

# RAYMOND LEVY

Copyright © 2012 Raymond Levy

All rights reserved.

ISBN:     1478224444

ISBN 13: 9781478224440

*To Flora and Max, who were in my thoughts throughout the writing of this book, written to tell them about the roots of their mysterious grandfather.*

# Acknowledgements

The idea of writing this book arose from an exchange of emails with my daughters Simone Dawood and Tanya Cohen during a return visit to Cairo. Ayhan Dawood provided me with photographs during the enjoyable trip we had together. Waleed Fawzi guided me through the mysteries of Word and kept me up to date with political developments in Egypt. Francine Loza was a constant source of tips and introductions I had entertaining encounters and meals with Nasser Loza, who also advised me on the transcription of Arabic letters.

Carmen Weinstein invited me to the historic rededication of the Maimonides Synagogue and a visit to the Bassatine Cemetery. Loutfiya and Michael Haag allowed me to join them on an illuminating visit to Alexandria. Talaat Badrawi kept me up to date with events in Cairo. Many friends and relatives read early manuscripts and made helpful suggestions. Amongst these were Amon Cohen, Claudia Roden, Ellis Douek, Johnny Bassili, Robin Jacoby, Suzy Benghiat and others too numerous to mention. My most prominent and constant inspirers have been the people of Cairo, Um el Dunya. Tessa Kilgour kindly proof read the text and retyped my manuscript. My wife, Aykan, held my hand patiently as I struggled through different versions of the text.

# Contents

***Synopsis***     *ix*

***Introduction***     *xi*

***Chapter 1***
Zamalek     1

***Chapter 2***
Antikhana Street (Now Mahmoud Bassiouni)     9

***Chapter 3***
Al Azhar And Fatimid Cairo     15

***Chapter 4***
Fatimid Cairo And Some Cairene Madness     21

***Chapter 5***
Coptic Cairo And Fustat     25

***Chapter 6***
Jewish Cairo, Ben Ezra, Adly And Maimonides Synagogue     31

***Chapter 7***
The Restoration Of The Maimonides Synagogue     37

***Chapter 8***
The Karaite Synagogue Of Abbaseya And The Bassatine Jewish Cemeteries     43

***Chapter 9***
Sunday Lunch In Maadi     47

***Chapter 10***
A Psychiatrist Again?     51

*Chapter 11*
Pharaonic Cairo                                                                 55

*Chapter 12*
The Search For A Famous Soup                                                    61

*Chapter 13*
The Cafe Riche And Other Cafes                                                  65

*Chapter 14*
Shisha (Hookah) And Mazag                                                       69

*Chapter 15*
A Picnic At Qanater El Khayreya (The Dams Of Welfare)                           73

*Chapter 16*
Feloukas And Dahabeyas – Floating Palaces
   And Floating Brothels                                                        77

*Chapter 17*
La Belle Epoque                                                                 81

*Chapter 18*
A Rotary Club Breakfast                                                         85

*Chapter 19*
Ibn Tulun Mosque, The Gair Anderson Museum
   And The Islamic Museum                                                       89

*Chapter 20*
The Opera House And Museum Of Modern Art                                        91

*Chapter 21*
Waiting For Omar                                                                93

*Chapter 22*
Taxis As A Source Of Wisdom                                                     99

*Chapter 23*
An Alexandrian Interlude                                                        103

*Chapter 24*
Conclusion                                                                      107

# Synopsis

## MAMNOU' – A RETURN TO CAIRO BY RAYMOND LEVY

*M*amnou' in Arabic means 'forbidden'. The 'GH 'sound (ein), now sometimes transcribed as a '3' or an inverted comma when at the end of a word, is produced by a gargling motion of the vocal chords. It was a word I frequently encountered during several nostalgic personal visits to my native Cairo in the last two years. It was used with different intonations: usually matter of fact, sometimes with a puzzled smile, rarely with rigid authoritarianism, and seldom with blind and uncontrollable anger. Its ambiguity encapsulates the paradox that is Egypt today. It is, in many ways, a metaphor for Cairo – a chaotic but occasionally restricted City which is, nevertheless, intriguing, friendly and amusing, though it can also be infuriating and puzzling to those who do not know it.

I retired from my chair of Old Age Psychiatry at the Institute of Psychiatry of King's College, London, and consultant at the Maudsley Hospital in 1996 and have, since then, devoted my time to travel, polishing my foreign languages, playing tennis and learning to scuba dive.

I was born in Egypt which I left in 1951 to study Medicine in Edinburgh where I spent ten years and moved to London in 1961. I have lived in London for the past 50 years. My parents, who spent their whole life in Egypt were expelled during the Suez crisis of 1956. My first return to Cairo was for a congress 30 years after my departure and I have since returned on numerous occasions for professional reasons and holidays. In this book

I describe incidents, conversations, thoughts and observations made during several nostalgic personal visits in the last two years to the Cairo of my youth. These have triggered memories of a vanished world.

I describe my impressions of the areas where I previously lived, studied and played, my encounters in Pharaonic, Muslim, Christian and Jewish Cairo, together with vignettes of famous cafes, meals alone and with Egyptian friends, and a unique literary luncheon in the historic Cafe Riche where my father played backgammon – and was still remembered by an elderly waiter. The book ends with observations on the contrast between rising fundamentalism in a City which is busy restoring synagogues, churches and monasteries, but whose youth is mainly ignorant of the long and uninterrupted presence of Jews in their country and have ceased to know the difference between Jew and Israeli. As I was in Egypt both before and after the latest 'Tahrir Revolution' I conclude with some final comments on the current political situation in Egypt.

The book concentrates on people and places, rather than on tourist sites, and attempts to give the reader a flavour of what Cairo is like today. The form which I have chosen to set it was to go to a famous or not so famous place, engage in conversation with a passer-by and report it, together with a description of the place and a flashback to earlier days of its existence. It is a cross between a tourist guide, a view of Cairo and a memoir.

# Introduction

*I* was born in Cairo at 5pm on the hottest day of 1933. The event was not reported in the Personal columns of The Times which did, however, have the following entry: 'Baron Arild Rosenkrantz's Exhibition of pictures is being kept open by request at the Cooling Galleries, 92 Bond Street'. I am delighted by the fact that I came out at 5pm as five has a special significance in Arabic. It represents the hand of Fatma and is definitely a lucky number. 'Khamsa u Khamastashar' (5 and 15) is used as an expression indicating good luck. On the other hand, in Spanish, it is the hour of death in a bullfight. 'A la cinque de la tarde', either the bull or the toreador gets it. Just as well that I am not superstitious.

It was said that my mother made such a fuss that the good Docteur Malartre, our general practitioner, very much a 'vieille France' man, lost his temper and flung all the instruments away. As a result, I grew up as an only child. Our family was Jewish– lite. Sephardi (Spanish) of mixed background. My father Chemtov dit (alias) Gaston, according to his passport, was born in Cairo, as were his father David and probably his grandfather, Scialom, son of Mordochai Levy. Somewhere along the way we must have had Algerian antecedents which resulted in our acquiring French nationality under the Loi Cremieux. This was instigated by Cremieux, a French Jewish minister who took the advantage of France's concern at its low population growth compared with that of Germany, to bestow French nationality on all Jews of Algerian ancestry, since Algeria was then not a true colony but an integral part of Metropolitan France. There were unforeseen consequences for me, notably the difficulty I had in giving up my French nationality when I was called up for

National Service in Constantine during the Algerian War. This drove me to seek British nationality, thus avoiding both National Service and the war in which I would have had to serve as a non-medical conscript.

Of David, I have vivid memories of a distinguished looking gentleman with a white moustache who wore a 'tarbouche'. In later years he would have an armchair put out in the street and would watch the world going by, whistling admiringly at attractive young women. There also were complaints of bottom-pinching from the nurse who looked after him. His wife, Fanny Arditi, who died young, hailed from the Ottoman Empire (Salonica) and was the last in our family to be fluent in Ladino Spanish (the language of Sephardi Jews). My father only had a few choice sayings he could remember such as 'The cucumber got up and hit the gardener' roughly equivalent to 'Teaching your grandmother to suck eggs' or 'You left me like a fart in a bath' to someone who did not turn up for an appointment.

Gaston was a forceful, somewhat explosive person and emotional person. He could break out into maniacal laughter but equally lose his temper easily or burst into tears very easily - a feature which became more marked in his later years. He could also be very witty, with quick repartie, for instance when in Paris after his expulsion from Egypt, he would always refuse to give the fierce little ladies who sat outside public lavatories any money. When they shouted "Service, Monsieur" after him, he would reply "Pourquoi? Est ce que vous me l'avez tenue?" ("Why? Have you held it for me?"). A dapper man, he always dressed meticulously, had his clothes made by the Armenian tailor, Chaljian, who dressed King Farouk. Equal care was taken over his shirts, shoes and socks which were all made to measure. He always had a prodigious collection of ties, as I did in my early adulthood. In season, he would wear a carnation in his button hole with some water in a pencil-shaped silver container hooked behind the lapel. Although bald, he would allow a lock of hair to grow on the side and stick it over the bare part of his head with a type of macassar called 'gomina', like Jackie Charlton, the footballer, in his day. During the time he held the shop at the old

## Introduction

Shepheard's Hotel, he developed an interest in Persian carpets and in China about which he became an expert. He collected white Chinese pottery of certain periods. Apart from the odd carpet, which could be folded up in a suitcase, all his collections remained behind in Cairo when my parents were expelled. He knew everybody and was hailed wherever he went, something which went on even in his impoverished state in Paris after their expulsion from Egypt.

He was secretive about his past and that of his family, so that getting information about our antecedents was a difficult task. "Ca n'a aucune importance", he would exclaim. I found out only indirectly of the link with the antique shop in Shepheard's, owned by him in partnership with his father, the source of his knowledge of Persian carpets and Chinese pottery. At one time, he had owned a soap factory and later, as an inveterate gambler, he took a particular interest in horse-racing. As the latter was illegal at the time, this might have explained his secretiveness. His gambling was compulsive and he would even play 'odds or evens' with pistachio sellers outside his favourite cafes. He always ended the loser as he would not collect his due of pistachios when he won.

Later, he bought or built properties. The large building in central Cairo where I was born which was like the now famous 'Yacoubian Building', popularised in El Aswany's novel, belonged to him, as did the smaller but smarter building we moved to in the plush suburb of Zamalek later. He was always very well-liked and respected particularly as he would go out of his way to be helpful. In spite of his short fuse, he could be extremely patient and persistent, particularly in his dealings with public authorities whom he would pester gently for weeks on end until he got the permit or document sought for at the time. He would take on these tedious tasks for other people sometimes against his own interests. "Why do I take on these bloody chores?" He would ask. Success would usually follow his efforts but, if it did not, he would blame himself for days. This skill later got me into Edinburgh University and got me out of having to serve in the Algerian war.

Gaston had an older brother, Edmond, a younger one, Maurice, and a young sister, Emilie. Although not the oldest, he always acted as head of the family.

My mother, Esther, was typical of the ladies of her generation. She was also very chic in appearance, gregarious and idle. With little interest in world affairs, she used to spend her time at parties and card games. Although she behaved as a bit of a spoilt child, she was popular with her friends and family but she contributed little but frustration to my upbringing which was taken on by my Slovenian nanny, Christina Sever. She was not much of a mother to me but was well-meaning. She was asphyxiatingly possessive with the irritating habit of rifling through my drawers to check on any relationships I had with girls who might not be 'suitable' and 'de bonne famille'. Later, when I was in Edinburgh, she always asked for packets of fruit jelly before we were due to meet. When asked for the flavour, she would 'tout mais pas lime' ('anything but lime'). The jellies were always an important part of an Egyptian buffet and the fact that the packets came from Britain gave them an added 'cachet'. As her knowledge of the geography of the British Isles was vague, she would get anxious if bad weather struck Wales or other distant parts of Britain. She would dash off a telegram saying 'Inquiets. Cablez nouvelles' ('Anxious. Send news by telegram'). I may be too hard on her as others always told me that she was essential to Gaston's survival.

Esther too was born in Cairo of Syrian parents from Aleppo. Both her father Rafoul (Raphael) and her mother, Salha, hailed from there. I have few memories of Rafoul , who died when I was young. I was protected from attending his funeral but later found his tomb by chance in the Cairo Jewish Cemetery on one of my recent visits. Salha (or Nonna Bigio as I knew her) was a miniscule lady who spoke Syrian Arabic dialect and broken French. She lived to a ripe old age during which she had a brief psychotic illness in the course of which she spoke to the television and addressed an imaginary person called Rachel. She responded rapidly and well to medication and she never required hospital treatment. She was a superlative cook and passed her skills on

## Introduction

to her cook, Ahmed, but unfortunately not to her daughter who inevitably had to do some cooking after their expulsion from Egypt. Esther learnt one or two recipes which she would cook after various telephone consultations with friends and relatives. She was good at some selected items liked stuffed vine leaves with tamarind, which was a speciality.

Esther was one of seven children, two of whom remain alive – my uncles Albert in Milan and Joseph (known as Zozo) in Sao Paulo. Her older sister, Marie, left Egypt before World War II and lived in Paris during the occupation. She was denounced by neighbours and sent to Drancy Concentration Camp, generally considered as a staging post for Auschwitz, but she somehow escaped this fate and would not speak of her experiences there other than saying that many women had their finger-nails ripped off. She was an unusual character who warrants a book to herself. She, too, had a psychotic illness when she believed that she was being bugged by her ex-husband, Simon Sisso, who was, she believed, hand-in-glove with President de Gaulle. She barricaded herself in her flat and had to have a compulsory admission to hospital necessary. Her condition responded well to anti-psychotic medication and she was discharged home back to her elderly lover. During Marie's hospitalisation, her lover's wife kept asking my mother when her sister would be out as she resented having her husband around all the time! After her lover's death, she soon found another man in his eighties. On being asked by mother whether he was Jewish, she replied "I don't know whether he is Jewish but he is circumcised!"

We were well–off, but not outrageously so by foreign middle class standards in Egypt. We nevertheless had a cook (from Southern Egypt), a servant (invariably a Nubian), a gardener, a chauffeur and, of course, my nanny, Christina, who came from the small town of Prvacina near Gorizia in what was then Yugoslavia. She was one of group of Slovenians who came to Egypt during the 19th and 20th century. They first came during the building of the Suez Canal and continued to be a presence until the late1950's. They are now attracting academic attention of Slovenian scholars and are known as 'Alexandrinke'. They are said to have numbered between 4,800 and 6,000. Some are now buried in Egypt and have become the subjects of numerous Ph.D theses and a very moving film.

I spoke French at home and Arabic in the street. I learnt Arabic, at first from our servants and from our redoubtable chauffeur, Abdu al Sawak, who also taught me to drive my first car, a war-time jeep and to joke with other drivers. This was later augmented by lessons at Victoria College from Yousef Effendi, Tewfik Effendi and the very strict Dabgh Effendi, rumoured to be an early member of the Muslim Brotherhood and by Ali el Gazzar, a teacher who gave me private lessons at home. Abdu, the chauffeur, had some favourite taunts such as "Dakhel fe reglak shoka?" ("Have you a got a spine in your foot?") shouted at drivers who did not follow the mad pace of Cairo traffic. Although my nanny spoke both Italian and Slovenian (a variant of Serbo Croat), I refused to speak Italian because of my opposition to Mussolini. Italian must, nevertheless, have been recorded somewhere in my brain as it later came back in a fluent but non grammatical form. Following recent courses it has nearly become both correct and fluent. Of Slovenian I only learnt some greetings, some swear-words ('driek na spici') meaning 'shit on a stick' being typical) and words connected with food. Unlike some of my contemporaries, I do not remember any songs. Occasionally, Christina would take me to the Yugoslav Club where I first tasted tripe. Sometimes, I would go with her to the Greek Catholic church which must have followed a service which was closest to the Slovenian one. This was my first contact with Christianity. After World War II, she had the choice of an Italian or Yugoslav nationality. She opted for the former and went to Rome where she married. It is my constant regret that I lost sight of her though she kept in touch with my parents by post.

I started my schooling at the French 'Cours Morin' but during World War II and, following a row with the Vichy French consul (Egypt was not then officially at war with France) who was our neighbour, my father decided that France was 'finished' and I was transferred to the English Gezira Preparatory School and then to Victoria College, where I was a day pupil. Because

## Introduction

the food consisted largely of stews and over-boiled cabbage, my cousin and I had food delivered by the son of the local florist who cycled across Cairo to deliver more acceptable repasts in 'gammelles', a bit like Indian 'Tiffin boxes'.

My childhood and adolescence were happy and carefree. I was something of a 'goody-goody' child and given as an example to my infuriated and spoilt younger cousin, Jean. At one time, my father - thinking that I was not aggressive enough - got me to take boxing lessons at home. I don't know why he chose boxing because he himself used to fence and was a member of the Royal Fencing Club. I do however remember trying a left hook on my teacher and being rewarded with a painful response which left my in tears. There was also a punching–ball attached to stout elastic cords hooked above and below to an archway leading to the entrance hall. I was to practise with this and skip very rapidly for a fixed time each day. I also learnt to swim early and played much tennis, first at the Maadi Sporting Club and later at the Tewfikiya Tennis Club (TTC), both remaining as favourite sports with me. As a teenager, I went to numerous parties where we danced to the sounds Latin- American, French and Italian popular music. I learnt enough Hebrew to have a bar-mitzvah but, unfortunately, did not keep this up and have forgotten the little Hebrew I knew. My parents did not keep a 'kasher' (Sephardi pronunciation of kosher) house, something that was the norm amongst their friends. We celebrated the main Jewish festivals like Passover, Rosh ha Shana (New Year) and fasted on Yom Kippur, though in my early teens I developed the habit of meeting my friend Loic Hemsy for a taameya (falafel) sandwich at lunch time so that, when the fast was broken, it was always remarked that "Raymond supporte le jeûne trés bien" ("Raymond takes the fast in his stride"). My other recollection of this period was the sumptuous Syrian Passover meals prepared first by my grandmother and, later, by her Egyptian cook Ahmed who came to surpass her culinary skills. This was usually attended by a vast number of uncles, aunts and cousins. Unusually, in a non-observant family, my mother would light a candle-wick stuck in a piece of cork floating in a glass of water with oil on top on Friday nights. This was invariably kept on top of an antique bookcase in front of a china pot in our drawing room. It became an object of some fascination for me when I took up photography after having received a 'Rolleycord' camera as a birth-day present. I did well at school usually sharing top position in most subjects with Loic Hemsy. After completing my 'A' levels we set out for the UK to find a medical school as I was set on a medical career. In Egypt then, only Montpellier and Edinburgh were considered Universities worth going to for Medicine. I wrongly thought that there was no Medicine in Oxford where my father thought he could pull strings. I was unsuccessful in getting a place in a London medical school in spite of an attempt to invoke the help of the Liberal Jewish peer, Lord Samuel. We were told that Edinburgh, which I favoured, was full but my father insisted on taking me to see the Dean and telling him, while I cringed in a corner, what a good boy I was and how, if I was accepted, would eventually bring honour to Edinburgh. By sheer luck, the Dean was Sir Sydney Smith, who was also Professor of Forensic Medicine and had worked for years for the Cairo police, which was then a common thing to do for ambitious forensic pathologists who wanted get a lot of practice in dissecting bodies which were in abundance in Egypt because of the numerous murders of women who had been considered to have dishonoured their peasant families. This proved another successful intervention of my father's negotiating skills.

So Edinburgh it was. Quite a shock for a spoiled 18-year old from Cairo, particularly because I was deposited in a strict boarding house at a time when rationing was still in force. Only one bath a week was allowed and one had to feed shillings in the meter to get some heat. However, I soon adapted, moved to more liberal digs run by a Pole and his blonde wife and came to like Edinburgh where I remained for ten years, taking my medical degree, the MRCP Ed (Member of the Royal College of Physicians of Edinburgh, a PhD in neurophysiology and marrying Katherine Logie, who was in my year at medical school. Our children Simone and Tanya were both born in Edinburgh.

## Introduction

As soon as I became a doctor, I was called up for French National Service which would have involved fighting in the Algerian War - not something I relished, particularly as my British Medical qualifications were no longer acceptable in France following a new law passed when I was in my third year. I would have had to serve in the ranks. I, therefore, applied, eventually successfully, for British Nationality - not without some amusing interviews in the Police Department of Explosives, Dangerous Drugs and Aliens where I thought I was being asked whether I suffered from bed-wetting when it was the interviewer who was trying to find out about the condition which affected his son. As by that time, National Service had been abolished in the UK, I escaped the army altogether. Getting rid of my French nationality was more of a problem and was only achieved by persistent lobbying by my father. However, it required a special act in the National Assembly to achieve this. It was essential to cease to be French as I would otherwise have been considered a deserter and would not have been able to visit my parents who were, by then, in Paris after their expulsion from Egypt during the Suez War. Again, by chance, my father found that the Minister's secretary was the daughter of an ex-Cairo drinking pal.

During my University days my parents remained in Cairo where they intended to end their days continuing to live a comfortable life there. However, their plans were cut short by the disgraceful Franco-British attack orchestrated by the then British Prime Minister, Anthony Eden, resulting in the Suez War of 1956 and President Nasser's expulsion of all British and French citizens and other foreign Jews with a sequestration of all their properties. My parents, therefore, left Cairo for Paris where they adapted remarkably well to their straitened circumstances. They departed with £50 each and the few carpets they were able to fold into their suitcases. They never returned and had no intention of doing so after what they considered the harsh treatment they had received. However, like many of my generation, particularly those who left relatively early and did not go directly through the process of expulsion, I remained nostalgic for Egypt.

My fellow exiles and I sublimated our nostalgia through the search for Middle Eastern food which was then very uncommon in London. We fell back on Claudia Roden who, after an artistic training at St Martin School of Art, started to collect recipes from her mother's friends which had to be tested out before entering into the first edition of 'Middle Eastern Food'. We lived the book as it was being written.

When in 1979, Sadat took Egypt into a peace with Israel, it became possible for nostalgic Cairo Jews to visit Egypt. Although everyone advised me not to do so as the country had changed so much that I would be disappointed, in 1981, I took the opportunity of a World Psychiatric Association International Symposium to return to Cairo and to combine this with a first exploration of my native city.

I was not disappointed and subsequently returned on numerous occasions both to Cairo and to different parts of the country. On my arrival at the Nile Hilton, I found Professor Ahmed Okasha in heated conversion with a group of Israeli psychiatrists who had crossed Sinai in a minibus. When he saw me, he urged me to intervene and explain to them that they could not be welcomed as a delegation but only as individuals. Participants were listed on the programme with the country they came from between brackets. The same was applied to the Israelis who chose to present papers. I explained to the Israelis that they were pushing their luck. Their one speaker was listed on the official programme with Israel after his name, in spite of the fact that his presentation was not really directly related to the theme of the Symposium. I was not part of a British delegation and no one else was. Their presence in Cairo represented an unbelievable progress and they should not ask for more. In the event, when the Israeli speaker approached the podium three young female psychologists wearing the Hejab (unusual at the time) got up and walked out. When I later spoke to them they said that they were feminists and Islamist, and that they disapproved of the peace which President Sadat had signed. For me, it was the first time I had seen middle class professional Egyptian ladies with covered heads.

## Introduction

My trip was most enjoyable and turned out to be the first of many. In 2009 – 2011, after one of my five visits - the last being in March 2011 soon after the 'Tahrir Square' demonstrations started - I found that I had written so much of what I was experiencing in e-mails to family and friends that I began to toy with the idea of putting it all in a book. The form I chose to set this in was to go to a famous or not-so famous place, engage a local in conversation and report this together with the setting and flashbacks from my earlier times in that particular location - a cross between a tourist guide, a view of Cairo today and a memoir.

# Chapter 1

# ZAMALEK

We lived at 11 Abul Feda Street in the smart inner suburb of Zamalek on the island of Gezira. According to Samir Rafaat's' Cairo – the Glory Years' one interpretation of the name is that it is the plural of the Albanian or Ottoman of 'zamlok' meaning a 'straw hut ', referring to the huts used by fishermen living in Bulak. Another is that it is a corruption of the Arabic 'zoumolk' meaning 'asset owner'. Other interpretations will, no doubt, emerge. When my father decided to get it built, the architect told him that the muddy surface of the banks of the Nile would only support two-and-a-half floors and a roof garden. When I returned many years after our exile, I found that it had become a 16-floor hotel with the extra floors piled on to the remaining flats. At Number 5 was the house of Om Kalthoum, the 'Edith Piaf' of the Middle East. On previous visits to Cairo I had combined tourism with clinical and academic pursuits and had usually been put up at the Marriott Hotel located in what had previously been the Loutfallah Palace, built in 1869 on the orders of the Khedive Ismail in preparation for the visit of Empress Eugenie to Egypt. It was later owned by the Loutfallahs, whose wealth was squandered by a manic-depressive member of the family in a euphoric spending spree.

On this occasion, I was paying for myself and elected to avoid 5* luxury, which was just as well, as I decided to stay in the more modest 16-floor Om Kalthoum Hotel also located in Abul Feda Street and built on the site of the singer's house after the opening of a museum in her name on the Island of Rodah. I would therefore be in our street but not in our old building. The idea of staying in 'our street' obviously appealed and though the hotel looked, at first, like a monstrosity, it was comfortable, had very helpful and friendly staff, many pictures of its previous occupant and was conveniently situated for what I planned to be the mother of all nostalgic journeys. It was occasionally irritating when simple things did not work but it had a charm all of its own and I have since made it my Cairo base. When I return, I always get a touchingly warm reception from the policeman at the door and then from the concierge who must have wondered what this elderly Arabic-speaking foreign buffer was doing in Cairo. They never asked and I never explained, except to say that I used to live along the road.

My first step was to pay another visit to our house along the road. As I explained earlier the three-floor building put up by my father had become the 16-floor Dutch-owned Flamenco Hotel although the first three floors remained intact. On an earlier visit in 1981, I had actually visited our flat, then occupied by relatives of an officer in the Egyptian Army who had had it allocated to him in a lottery following my parent's expulsion from Egypt in 1957. I had met the officer's sister by chance in London. This was indeed an extraordinary coincidence. I had come across a young Egyptian student called Ahmed el Bahtimi at the Maudsley Hospital and thought him somewhat homesick, I invited him for Sunday lunch and we served Middle Eastern food. He was delighted and a few weeks later said that his parents were in London and wanted to meet me. I met them for tea and found his father to be a distinguished 'ancient regime' type who had been the curator of the Agricultural Museum in Cairo - the first museum I ever visited in childhood, when we learnt about the growing of cotton. He and I played backgammon as we talked, in English, of the old days. After the game, I turned to his wife who had been standing aside as she did not speak any English. She asked: "Whereabouts in Cairo did you live? "Zamalek", I replied. "My brother also lives in Zamalek", she replied. We gradually narrowed down the area which is about the size of Chelsea and I had the uncanny feeling that her brother must be in our flat. After some exchanges, it turned out that I was right! This brought tears of nostalgia to my eyes. My emotions were misunderstood by the mother who apologised for upsetting me. I explained to her that unlike my parents, I had not personally experienced the expulsion from Egypt. I was not upset but very moved.

During the later visit, I was outside our old building trying to revisit our flat. The bawab (caretaker), a 'Saidi' from Upper Egypt, was sitting outside with his cousin and I told him a bit about the story of the building which he had known for only ten years. When I asked to visit our flat he told me that it would not be possible as the occupants were asleep. As it was 11am, I took this with a pinch of salt as a first example of the Mamnou' (forbidden) phenomenon. On a subsequent visit, I was able to gain access to the flat again and to meet the current owner who was a son of the man who occupied it first. He worked in the Nile valley where he made mozzarella, not from buffalo milk, as I expected, but from cow's milk which he said was cheaper. He was puzzled at the fact that I spoke Arabic and was unaware of the previous existence of a Jewish community, some of whose members had lived in Egypt since pharaonic days and others who were later arrivals in the centuries following their expulsion from Spain in 1492. He asked me for the difference between Jews and Israelis and I repeated the standard lesson I use on these occasions.

The flat itself had hardly changed which was not surprising as the new owner had made enquiries about the previous occupants and tried to keep the flat as near-unchanged as possible. The exception was the fact that the windows of my previous bedroom were blocked by the Flamenco Hotel which had been extended in what had been the building's garden and the entrance to the underground car park. Both had disappeared. Once again, this was very moving but less so than on my first visit in 1981 when I had met his mother.

I continued my 'promenade' of Zamalek by walking to the Aquarium Garden which I sometimes went to as a child with Christina. It was totally unchanged. Even the fish were there, though difficult to see because of the green mould that had grown on the glass of the tanks It was a public holiday for the Coptic Christmas and the garden was full of children of all ages. A teenager approached me and asked "Are you Muslim?" "No". "What are you then?" "A bit of this and that. It is complicated". "Do you pray?" "No, do you?" "Yes, five times a day. Do you really never pray?" At this stage he seemed so puzzled and upset that I felt I should compromise with my atheist principles. "Well, very rarely, I do pray". "When do you pray?" "Well, for instance, if I want my football team to win". Big smile. From then on there was no more talk about religion. Only football and girls. "What is your football team? Manchester United? Chelsea?" "No", I replied, "when I am in London it is Arsenal when I am in Cairo it is Nadi al Ahly". I had guessed which club he supported. He beamed now and called his friends. "Chaps, there's an Ahly supporter here from London". Fifteen boys turned up and I asked them to line up like a football team which they did while pushing one boy away. "Why won't you let him in?" "He is not an Ahlawi. He supports Zamalek!". I whispered to the boy that I would take a separate photo of him later. They all surrounded me and asked questions about football in the UK. I pointed to a sign that said that it was Mamnou' to play with a ball. "Why is it Mamnou'? I asked. They looked surprised and puzzled "Maybe because of the gardener". The latter approached, looking at me suspiciously. "Can I help you?" "It's all right", they all chimed. "He is with us". I had gained acceptance from this rumbustious group of young Muslims.

I left the garden and feeling peckish, bought myself something to eat. I sat on the bank eating my taameya (falafel) sandwich on the banks of the Nile by some moored dahabeyas (house boats). In Cairo, no one uses the term 'falafel' . The equivalent 'taameya' is made with fava beans not the tasteless chick peas which have invaded the world via Lebanon and Israel. It is usually eaten in or with pitta – like bread which is made rougher and more tasty bread called 'Esh Baladi'. Those who live in London will find this delicacy in only one place – the small Ali Baba restaurant in Ivor Place off Baker Street. To get good service one has to declare one's Ahly-supporter credentials.

Having finished my sandwich, I felt that it was time for a bit of culture, so I went on to the Sakia Cultural Centre which did not exist in my day. It is located on Abul Feda Street next to the main thoroughfare of Zamalek's 26th July Street previously King Fouad Street. Outside the entrance was displayed a widely used and ingenious device dating from pharaonic times called the 'sakia' which was one of the earliest systems used to raise Nile water and irrigate the parched earth around it. It had been the subject of many a thesis and had been used as an example of 'intermediate technology' in a UNESCO-funded project run by Jean Gimpel (of the famous art-dealing family) and Amr Baghdadi, a young engineer who built miniature replicas to show people in other countries who did not know the technique but could copy it using their common sense. Amr and I subsequently became great friends. In the garden, a group of young women were collecting money for the people of Gaza who were then experiencing the combined effects of the Israeli bombing and siege during the retaliations following the Hamas and Hezbollah release of rockets on to Southern Israel. This was the only time I saw any manifestation of feeling over the plight of the Palestinians. Most of my questions were responded to by a shrug of the shoulders which seemed to say "We have our own problems of day to day survival and don't have time for this". The earnest young women collecting did not seem to be raising much interest. I bought a scarf and a biro, and entered the cultural centre. There was an exhibition by a Mozambique painter and on a large TV screen, at the other end, a documentary on a new singer called 'Salma'. I asked for a DVD or CD of her songs, but they did not have any. Judging by the activities in the leaflet I took on my way out, this must have been a quiet day.

I continued my explorations of the back streets of Zamalek in the search for a restaurant where I could have Molokhia (a traditional Egyptian soup) that evening and found one in Taha Hussein Street near the President Hotel. Molokhia, sometimes called 'mallow' or 'Jew's mallow' on the rare occasions when it is known in the west, is a green leaf looking something like spinach but producing a glutinous green soup which was eaten in ancient Egypt and is portrayed on the walls of tombs. Recipes differ but all include a rabbit, lamb or chicken stock, the leaves and a mixture of pounded and fried garlic and coriander seeds known as 'takleya'. It has been a staple in the diet of the Egyptian peasant from time immemorial, but is not always to the taste of westerners because of its glutinous nature. The restaurant did serve an acceptable lamb-based form of the dish but I had to endure the TV which was showing an Ahli v Suez football game and all the waiters were glued to the box. Ahly won 3/1.

An agreeable evening but not one which I had envisaged. On leaving the restaurant I wandered around the streets of Zamalek.

While walking around I was struck by a flamboyant neo-gothic building, unusual for this part of Cairo. It turned out to be the Faculty of Music of Helwan University. Beside that stood another less unusual building with a large garden where attractive young people were drawing. It was 'The Faculty of Arts' of the same university. I tried to photograph it not very successfully through the railings and decided that I needed to gain access to the grounds but I met with an implacable Mamnou' at the entrance. On my way back to my hotel, I noticed that there was a useful internet cafe just behind the Flamenco Hotel. It became a favourite haunt for me during the rest of my stay.

Back at my hotel, I sat down at the trendy Coffee Pot Cafe for a mango juice. It was a warm evening and I sat outside. At a nearby table were four very attractive young women with no head scarves and one man, all smoking designer shishas (water pipes). I realised that I had to ring my friend, Francine, to organise Sunday lunch at her house in Maadi but being without the right SIM card in my mobile, I asked the young man whether I could borrow his. He kindly agreed to do so.

While speaking to Francine, I asked her if Omar Sherif was in town. We had been together at school and acted together in 'Le Malade Imaginaire,' where I was Docteur Diafoirus. One of the girls approached me and asked: "Do you know Omar Sherif?" she asked. "Yes, I was at school with him. I have not seen him for years but since he is now in Cairo I will try to arrange to meet him". My status with the young women rose immediately. One of them insisted on giving me her phone number so I could ring her if I was meeting him.

# Chapter 2

# ANTIKHANA STREET (NOW MAHMOUD BASSIOUNI)

Before moving to Zamalek we lived on the 4th floor of this seven-floor building resembling the now famous 'Yacoubian Building' which was where I was born. As the name Antikhana implies (House of Antiquities), it is located close to the Cairo Museum and is crossed by Champollion (Decipherer of Hieroglyphs) Street. It is also a stone's throw from the famous Art Deco Patisserie Groppi located in Soliman Pacha Square, now renamed Talaat Harb Square. (Soliman Pacha was an officer in Napoleon's army who later became a general went native and converted to Islam).

The building had belonged to my father and he had a variety of tenants. On our floor were our friends the Benghiats whose son, Fred, remained my closest friend until his death from pancreatic cancer some years ago. As children, we used to amuse ourselves by peeing on people in the street from his balcony and bouncing 'petards' (bangers) off the 'Pension Suisse' on the building opposite. We never got arrested. On the 5th floor above us was my father's sister, Emilie, her husband Edouard Amiel and their children, Maryse and Jean. As Edouard died young my father assumed a semi-paternal role, so that Jean was the closest to being the brother I never had. Also in the building was the Consul for Vichy France (Egypt was not officially at war with France). There was also a man suffering from what I now realise must have been Parkinsonism who use to descend the stairs at an uncontrolled rate making everyone fearful that he would fall and break his neck, and a nursing sister known as Sister Rose who would be called upon to give injections and cupping which was still in use when I was young. Other antiquated medicaments included the red 'mercurochome tincture' as an antiseptic for surface wounds. It had the advantage of not stinging unlike the more usual tincture of iodine. For mouth ulcers it was common to use 'methylene blue' which has long been abandoned for humans but is occasionally used for horses. Poultices of linseed or a substance called 'antiphlogistine' were also common and there were other old wives' beliefs such as eggs being bad for the liver and the eating of melons potentially deadly before entering the sea for a swim. For the most resistant aches in the limbs people sometimes resorted to a native bone setter called 'Barsoum el Megabaraty' who had a great reputation both amongst locals and amongst the middle class as a healer of last resort. I remember visiting him in my youth with 'tennis elbow'. His consulting room left much to be desired in terms of hygiene but, in compensation, was a lively and interesting sight. The important and good thing about him was that he knew when he could not cope with a problem and to suggest referral to a doctor. I remember leaving with a crepe bandage of doubtful cleanliness but it cured the 'tennis elbow'. The native bone setters are called 'Megabaraty'.

They are often consulted ether by those who cannot afford a doctor or when more traditional treatment has failed. They have to be considered within the main gamut of 'traditional medicine'.

## Antikhana Street (Now Mahmoud Bassiouni)

A more extreme local 'treatment' is the 'Zar' ceremony (basically a casting out of the devil) which is rarely performed nowadays. It involves ritual dancing with much twirling of the head and neck. It is usually favoured by women who might be suffering from what we would call 'psychosomatic' conditions if not out and out 'conversion' symptoms. It is sometimes performed during lunar eclipses to chase away the devils. In my early days in psychiatry, I heard that a ceremony was put on at great expense for the famous Dr William Sargent of St Thomas' who claimed to be an expert on exorcism and brain washing techniques. These fake ceremonies sometimes appeared in the films he showed and in his infamous book, 'Battle for the Mind'.

Back to our old building, I also remember an air-raid shelter which had been installed in the basement. Although Cairo was never bombed during the War, there were occasional air-raid alerts during which we would all assemble until the all-clear signal went on. Windows were also blacked out and there were warders going round saying 'Tafi nour' (Put out the lights). On the ground level there were two shops, one a florist whose son used to deliver our food when Jean and I were at school, the other a Greek grocer called Psilidis. It was from him that I learnt that 'Kalamata' olives were 'the best in the world'. The street outside was pretty active and there were a number of habitual characters whose shouts still resonate in my head when I think back. There was the 'Mounadi' (taxi rank manager) who used to shout "Yallah ya bringi" (Off you go first cab), the rag and bone-man whose call was "Roba Becchia" (a distorted Italian for old things) and, finally, the incense seller with "Titito, titito" miming a car driver and saying "Accelerateur, debreyage" (Accelerator, clutch). One man would walk along muttering "'Ya Rab Mit Alf Guiney" (God, give me 100,000 pounds). Someone like him is still there and the amount has not changed in spite of inflation and multiple devaluations of the Egyptian pound.

There was one cry that always stuck terror in my heart though I never knew what the man who shouted was selling. 'Marangon' was the word and I have since found out that it means 'carpenter' in Turkish. If I misbehaved, I was told that 'marangon' would be called and as a result would toe the line.

When I first revisited Cairo in 1981, 30 years after first leaving the building and the streets around it seemed smaller than I remembered and were endowed by a quality of unfamiliarity described by neurologists as the 'jamais vu' phenomenon. This feeling did not disappear until I set eyes on the statue of Saad Zaghloul across the bridge, when there was a sort of click in my head and everything seemed 'right'. On a later occasion, this feeling was not present, both these qualities were missing and everything looked of normal in size and really familiar. The building, which had seemed dilapidated the first time, had been partly restored by my second visit and the entrance, previously with a sandy floor, had regained its old marble floor or something like it. As I pushed open the front door I noticed that, very unusually, the bawab (caretaker) was a woman. I told her that I was born in one of the flats on the 4th floor and wished to visit it if possible. She looked very dubious but accompanied me to the ancient Otis (Otis and Roux-Combalusier seemed to have a monopoly lift. However, when we reached the 4th floor she refused to let me out clearly thinking that she had been wrong to let me in. I was unable to persuade her to let me out of the lift and visit the flat. We returned to the ground floor and left the building somewhat disappointed about this further Mamnou' but more accepting. I was dying to see our panelled hall where I took boxing lessons.

I crossed the road and walked along Champollion Street to the Midan Al Tahrir, a very large open square notoriously difficult to cross and now famous for the recent 'Spring Revolution'. I took the hairy crossing to the opposite side of the midan with hooting taxis barely missing me as I walked.

I first crossed over to the Cairo Museum which had dominated much of my youth and led to my casual interest in Egyptology. I always had a special feeling for the large and dusty museum, partly because I was born less than a mile away and partly because of my interest in codes and languages. Interestingly enough, in order to get to the museum from our house one passes by street named after Champollion, the great man who deciphered the

## Antikhana Street (Now Mahmoud Bassiouni)

Rosetta Stone. When I got to the museum, I had a nice surprise when passing Mariette's statue (founder of the Museum and originator of the libretto for Verdi's Aida) to buy my ticket, only to be asked whether I was an Egyptian or foreigner 'Masri walla Agnabi' (there is a large difference in price for the ticket between the two). I replied "Agnabi" indicating that I was a foreigner but the man at the ticket office said "You sound Egyptian" and gave me the cheaper ticket. I revisited the museum which had hardly changed and went to see Tut Ankh Amun's mummy with only its head and feet showing. I mused over the numerous myths about the Curse of the Mummy and promised myself to visit Highclere Castle, home of Lord Carnarvon, who had financed and supported Howard Carter's 12-year search for the tomb. The recent 'Downton Abbey' television series was shot at the Castle but I am ashamed to say that I have not yet visited it.

On emerging from the museum, I made my way towards the nearby art deco Kasr el Nil Bridge which is guarded by four splendid bronze lions. In the large space on my right, which had previously accommodated the British barracks, were the Arab League Building and the Nile Hilton Hotel. As I crossed the bridge towards the island of Gezira I was aware of the impressive statue of the nationalist leader Saad Zaghloul with the new opera complex behind him. To his left, as he faced me, were the elaborately decorated Andalusian gardens looking somewhat like a poor man's Alhambra and, to his right, the un-named gardens I used to go to nearly every day with my Slovenian nanny, Christina, who belonged to a Slovenian cohort of women who first came to Egypt at the time of the building of the Suez Canal. They were mainly employed as nannies to middle class families and have now become the subjects of these at the University of Llubliana. The gardens had large banyan trees which we used to climb. The sight of all this brought back a mass of old memories of my childhood including one which remains particularly vivid. There was a boy called Pussy Hamawi who thrust a pin into the eye of his consenting younger brother, an episode which now reminds me of the beginning of the film 'L'age d'or' (or is it 'Un chien andalou'?) directed by Bunuel and Dali.

I walked through the gardens to the other end which abuts on the Moukhtar Museum after the sculptor who had been very popular in the 1930's when his fame spread to Paris. He came to specialise in statues like that of Saad Zaghloul and others. His 'Le Reveil de l'Egypte' ('Egypt's Awakening') used to stand in a square on the road to the pyramids and I reminded myself that I should check to see if it still there (it is). Having visited the handsome display of his sculptures in the museum , I crossed the road to the opera complex with the Opera House itself donated by the Japanese – a granite building of neo-oriental appearance. In the grounds outside it stands a small Museum of Modern Art. All this brought memories of the old Opera House, commissioned for the opening of the Suez Canal and destroyed during a fire. It was there that I saw my first opera (very appropriately Aida) and numerous performances by the Comedie Francaise who used to perform every year as well as the 'The Old Vic' in its pre-National Theatre incarnation. I remember particularly a much applauded appearance of the great Louis Jouvet in 'Knock' and 'Le Malade Imaginaire'. Although Aida, with its libretto by Mariette Pacha, the Egyptologist and founder of the Egyptian Museum, was commissioned from Verdi for the opening of the Canal it was not ready in time and the Cairo Opera House opened with 'Rigoletto'.

Exhausted by all this reminiscence I felt I had had enough and took a taxi to my hotel.

# Chapter 3

# AL AZHAR AND FATIMID CAIRO

*H*aving started by visiting places of personal significance, I resumed my visits to places of more general interest and, particularly, to the Al Azhar Park which did not exist in my day and to the recent restorations of Fatimid Cairo around it.

During most of recent history, Egypt has been a bulwark for the Sunni interpretation of Islam but there was a time between 969 and 1106 when it was almost entirely Shia. That was a result of the Fatimid invasion from Tunisia. A good deal of the Islamic centre of the city including the Mosque of El Azhar, that bastion of Sunnism, was built by the Fatimids. This also applies to the main buildings of the Khan Khalili market, to the Bab el Zuela entrance into the old city and to the line of important mosques, madrassas caravanserais, hospitals and old houses along Al Muez Street leading to Bab el Nasr and Bab al Futtuh, the eastern gates which were traditionally the departure points for the pilgrimage to Mecca. This area of the city is currently being restored with funds from the Aga Khan Foundation which is also responsible for the building of a large park backing on the el Azhar mosque facing the Citadel and the Moccatam hills. The park is part of a master plan close to the heart of the Aga Khan who is funding and supervising a chain of schemes to make life for pleasant for people throughout the Muslim world. I was determined to see this park which I did not know and to have a look at the restorations to the Fatimid areas.

I set off on the 7th January 2010 which was the Coptic Christmas. I asked my favourite taxi driver to take me to el Azhar and was surprised to be told that it was closed for the Coptic Xmas! We therefore drove on to the only entrance of the park which was up a hill some distance away. That was also closed but due to open at 9am, ten minutes later. The entrance fee of seven Egyptian pounds (LE7) roughly equivalent to £1 at the time (the price is lower for Egyptians) seemed to me prohibitive for the average Cairene, though it must be said that the park is magnificent, offering superb views in every direction. Not surprisingly there was only a handful of middle class-looking visitors in suits. I walked around taking pictures and, as I approached one of the attractive neo-Ottoman looking new restaurants to photograph, a policeman stepped in front of me saying the fateful word 'Mamnou''. "Do you mean to say that it is not allowed to take any photos in the park? "No, it is only forbidden for restaurants. Otherwise, you can photograph to your heart's content". "What is special about restaurants?" I asked. He shrugged his shoulders and said "I have my orders It is Mamnou' Further along, I found a friendly-looking cafe. I sat down near an artificial lake and ordered a coffee. "Sorry, there is a minimum charge of LE35", said the apologetic waitress, "but you can have one at the bar". The cafe was totally deserted.

I continued my perambulations and was fascinated by a Fatimid–looking dome which I could see in the distance inside the old city walls. Unable to identify it, I made my way towards it hoping that I would find a gate out of the park at the Azhar – end or near it - but it became clear that none existed. However, Egypt being what it is, I found a gap in the park wall and was able to squeeze through into the old city and found myself in the old quarter of Darassa with the mysterious dome a few minutes' walk away. It turned out to be the Mamluk mosque of Al Aslam al Salihdar built in 1344 and, therefore, post–Fatimid but also currently subject to restoration by the Aga Khan Foundation and others. By that time, I was feeling hungry and seeing an ambulant taameya maker bought myself an ortas (paper cone) of six freshly made and hot taameyas with no bread as I was vainly trying to diet. Having finished these, I pushed on towards the fruit market and El Azhar to buy some tangerines known in Arabic as 'Youstafandi' short for Yousef Effendi, thought by some to refer to the Jewish man who first introduced the fruit to Egypt. As I was sitting on a canopy outside the venerable mosque picking at the deliciously juicy segments, I heard someone saying "Hey Mister" in English. "Don't hey mister me my dear fellow ", I replied in Arabic, "I am not a Khawaga (a somewhat derogatory term for a foreigner) I was born in this city". He was a tall man wearing casual sports clothes, leather jacket and designer Ray ban-type sunglasses. He told me he was called Fahd and was an unemployed guide. I explained, apologetically, that I did not need a guide. I was just walking about looking at the restorations. He said he was at a loose end and asked to join me in my walk. I wondered, for a while, whether this was some sort of scam but one look at the man reassured me and I decided to trust him. I did not regret it. We went to have some tea and a shisha and had a chat. He confirmed his name of Fahd, said he was 39, was married and had a five-year old child. His wife was also an under-employed guide, but French- speaking. His father was a Bedouin based in Sinai. He told me that he was a Sufi and when I expressed some surprise, he informed me that there were about 80,000 Sufis in Egypt. I spoke to him about my previous encounters with Sufis in Iran in 1972 when I stayed in a 'khanaga' (a sort of monastery and dormitory for itinerant dervishes). This was in Shiraz when I had interesting conversations with the Sufi Sheikh who was the only other occupant of the 'khanaga'. At that time, there was concern about hippies. Searching for a common language, I tried to address him in classical Arabic.

"Oh Sheikh. How do Sufis differ from 'hippies'?". After some thought, he replied "They seek. We have found". As I took snuff in those days, we discussed the therapeutic benefit of sneezing for the mad. Fahd was impressed by all this and recommended to me of a meeting of 'whirling dervishes' which was taking place that evening at 7.30 at the Wikala of Ghouri – a sort of converted Fatimid caravanserai, much used for cultural activities. As we chatted, he told me that he thought I must be Jewish. He was in fact, one of the few in Cairo to guess that I was Jewish. He explained to me that this was because his Bedouin father often took Israeli tourists through the Sinai desert and had often spoken to him on the days when "We all lived together in harmony, irrespective of religion".

"Do you need anything?" he asked. "Not really, but my daughter asked me to get some spices and there was one I could not find - 'Ras el Hanout' (this is a mixture which is mainly used in Morocco)". He asked where I had bought my spices and I pointed to a stall. "That' no good", he said. "When you buy spices, you must not go just anywhere. This is a fruit and vegetable market and the stall there is a general purpose spice shop. We have to go to the spice market". We walked through minute streets towards the Bab el Zuweila and found myself in a small spice shop owned by a friend of his. I asked for 'Ras el Hanut'. The owner replied "Ya bey, all the foreigners ask for that, but I must tell you that it is really a Moroccan mixture. There is an Egyptian equivalent called 'Bokharat'. It is a mixture of 35 spices and is quite expensive. We sell it by the gram". Fahd immediately interjected "Don't give us this bullshit. Raymond is not a 'khawaga' he is one of us". I left with 200g of the mixture and paid practically nothing for it,

"Is there anything else you need?" Fahd asked. "Yes. Can you recommend a place that makes good rabbit-based molokheya?" "That's easy", he says. "Come to dinner at my house tonight and my wife will make some for us". I thanked him profusely, told l him that I was busy and took his card as he was obviously very knowledgeable about the area and I might be able to recommend him to anyone coming to Cairo who was looking for a good and

## Al Azhar and Fatimid Cairo

witty guide. He reminded me of the dervish show which was on that night and we arranged to meet there if he happened to be going.

I had previously seen 'whirling dervish' shows in Iran, Turkey and Syria, and expected the sober appearance of the dervishes in white robes and tall black hats representing tombstones. The whirling was done with one hand pointing upwards and another to the floor. The music also struck me as somewhat mournful, reflective and inclined to be repetitive. Instead, the Egyptian version was exuberant and multicoloured. Flashy and gaudy patterns were produced as the individuals rotated, often for up to 45 minutes in the same direction. When they stopped they remained totally still with no unsteadiness. Here, the tall black hat was replaced was replaced by a white turban and the white robes by multicoloured ones. I was unable to determine whether this was because Egyptian Sufis belonged to a separate school or whether the traditional costume and ceremony had been adapted to suit the Egyptian personality. As Fahd was not there, I could not ask him but I subsequently found out that Egyptian Sufis belong to a separate sect, Fahd did not appear by the end of he evening and subsequent inquiries drew a blank. An email to the address he had given me was returned. I am sorry to have lost contact with him.

On the off chance that I might meet him again outside his 'beat', the El Azhar Mosque, I returned there some months later and had tea in his local cafe. I waited a good half hour but alas did not encounter him. In spite of this fact, I thought of the series of paradoxes before me. Here was I, an atheist Jew, waiting outside the holy of holies of the Sunni Muslim world-the fount of all orthodoxy, a mosque founded in the 10th century by a Shia dynasty (The Fatimids) for a guide who was the son of a Bedouin. The Azhar University, where previously only religion could be studied, had been widened in its remit by Nasser in an attempt to liberalise it. It is now possible to study such subjects as medicine and engineering but only in unisexual faculties. This division was thrown into relief some years previously when a male medical student had a sex change operation with the backing of the then Professor of Psychiatry and a Gynaecologist. The problem was 'Which Faculty should he attend?' This was resolved when the religious authorities judged the operation to have been illegal and moved to have the Professor of Psychiatry struck off.

After musing along these lines for an hour, I noticed a large well-dressed man smoking his shisha with evident pleasure. He did not seem in a hurry to rush away any where, so I engaged him in conversation. It emerged that he was an artisan specialised in the inlaid mosaic work so often seen on boxes and furniture sold in the Khan el Khalili. Though he realised that he was not about to make a sale, he insisted on taking me to his workshop to see his young son at work. He then told me that his daughter suffered from a congenital disorder (primary erythrocitic aplasia). Although aged in her twenties she was like a small girl and required constant medical attention with no hope of a cure in the current state of medical knowledge. He insisted on taking me to his nearby flat where I met his wife whose occupation involved the blending of local flower essences. We had a karkade (hibiscus infusion) together and he hailed me on my way with a promise on my part to find out European views on his daughter's condition which I later confirmed was truly untreatable at the time. I felt both sad and helpless, and hoped that he might perhaps have had a moment of relief in showing off his the English which he insisted on using with me.

# Chapter 4

# FATIMID CAIRO AND CAIRENE MADNESS

As I had not seen all I wanted to see the previous day, I returned to Fatimid Cairo via the main entrance of the Khan el Khalili market opposite the El Hussein Mosque. This is the area where a bomb was set off a few years ago, killing a French school girl and wounding others. My own visit was a few weeks earlier and there was no indication of any threat. The Fatimid drag with the-most-to-see is in El Muezz Street between Bab El Zuweila and Bab el Futuh. Fatimid has become a buzz word for good Islamic architecture in Cairo though, in all honesty, a good deal of what passes under that rubric was built after the end of this unusual Shia period and is, strictly speaking, Mamluk or later. Cynics say that the emphasis on the word 'Fatimid' (from Fatma the prophet's daughter) made it easier to obtain funds from the Ismaili families of successive Aga Khans whose movement was derived from Shiism.

It is said that at one time Cairo had many more gates, some say thousands. It is an important paradox that the three which survive Zuela, Nasr and Futuh were all associated with Armenian or Christian Anatolian architects but then Cairo is a city of paradox. My main reason for returning to this medieval area was to try to determine the structures of which the bimaristan or lunatic asylum formed a part. These hospitals which started to appear in the Muslim world in Iraq, Syria and Egypt around the 11th century AD, usually consisted of a mosque, a madrassa (coranic school), a general hospital and, often, a mental hospital, the bimaristan. The restored one, which I had previously visited in Aleppo, is now used to accommodate such events as dervish ceremonies, was built in the 11th century. The most carefully restored and easy to visit one was built much later in 1451 under Sultan Beyazid II in Edirne in Turkey and is referred to as the Kulliye of Beyazid II. It is in Edirne in Turkey near the Greek and Bulgarian borders. These places were typified by the humane treatment of the insane and the use of music, the sound of running water and the pleasant smell of jasmine, roses and other flowers at a time when, in the Christian west, such patients were kept chained or burnt as witches, they were totally unrestrained.

The Cairo representative of this movement is to be seen in the complex of Mansur al Qalawun which is slap in the middle of El Muezz Street. He was a Mamluk of Tartar or Mongol origin from the lower Volga. He became Sultan in 1279 and died in 1290 while giving siege to the crusaders in Acre. His mausoleum and madrassa are both in good condition but the medical section has been transformed into an ophthalmic hospital with no apparent trace of its previous use, although an Egyptian psychiatrist friend has told me that, by bribing the caretaker and a certain amount of nibble footwork, it is sometime possible to visit what are said to have been rooms used for the insane. The architecture of the complex formed a model for similar institutions in the Muslim world.

Further towards the north in the direction of Bab el Futuh is the gorgeously restored and grand Beit el Suheimy and other grand Mamluk houses, either restored or closed for restoration. They include Beit Uthman Katkhouda and Qasr Beshtak.

It should be said that the restorations are now being extended to Mamluke palaces, notably the 14th century Amir Taz which is located in the El Khalifa area near the Ibn Tulun Mosque.

This has been lovingly restored and includes a didactic display on the Mamlukes. When I visited, it had just opened and the space set aside for temporary exhibitions was occupied by a stunning and seldom displayed selection of Coptic art with several posters on the Copts – who they were, their beliefs and a history of the Desert Monasteries. A gem well-worth visiting. There were no tourists there but only a number of art students from the University of Helwan. Since they were all Muslims, this was a rare and touching example of inter-religious understanding.

After all this culture, I returned to the trendy 'Copper Pot' cafe to relax with a mango juice and to take more photographs of the designer shishas in use in this cafe. The place was packed full with no free tables. As I saw a young woman sitting alone smoking her shisha and working on her Apple computer, I asked if I could share her table she said "Of course" and went back to her work. I thought that the comparison between this environment and that of the more traditional shisha establishment where I had had my coffee in the morning would make an interesting photographic contrast. I proceeded to snap two Russians on my right, puffing away on their shishas and some young city slickers who were also playing backgammon. I then asked the girl with the' Apple' whether I could have her permission to photograph her. She refused and I put my camera away. Suddenly, out of nowhere ,came an irate manager shouting Mamnou', Mamnou' like a madman. I inquired from him what it is that was forbidden but he kept shouting Mamnou' I wanted to understand what it is that was Mamnou', but he was so beside himself that all he was capable of was to repeat the dreaded word. I said "OK I have ordered a mango juice, please cancel it and I will go". I got up. A man at another table shrugged his shoulders and said "This is Egypt" with a smile. As I made a move towards the door, a waiter pointed to another table that was now free. I told him angrily "Take that table and shove it up your manager's arse".

The next morning, still puzzled by this incident, I went back to the cafe to try and find out what sent the manager into a spin. The general consensus was that I sat at a table which was already occupied, something which is not done in Cairo today. I would not have done this in a traditional place but the cafe was so trendy and cosmopolitan and since the girl agreed I saw so harm in it. I was beginning to see the different faces of Mamnou'.

## Chapter 5

# COPTIC CAIRO AND FUSTAT

*T*he Copts, who constitute about 10% of the population of Egypt, are the Christians of Egypt. There are, of course, some Catholics, Maronites, Greek and Russian Orthodox Christians, Syrian Catholics & Syrian Orthodox and some Protestants but to all intents and purposes, the Copts are the Christians of Egypt. Indeed they could be said to be the Egyptians of Christ. The word 'Copt' is derived from the Arabic 'Qibt' which was in turn a transformation of the Greek 'Aegyptos'. Some say that it ultimately comes from the ancient Egyptian 'Hikuptah' meaning 'House of the Energy of Ptah', Ptah' being the religious name for Memphis. It is said that Mark, a Jewish shoemaker of Alexandria, brought Christianity to Egypt though evidence is scarce. It is, however, established that it came in 1st century AD to some Jews in Alexandria from where it spread to Cairo and that by the 3rd century, the Greek version of the Bible was already translated into the Coptic language. There is a relationship between the Coptic language and ancient Egyptian. In fact, Champollion's knowledge of the Coptic language may well have given him an edge in the race to decipher Egyptian hieroglyphs on the Rosetta stone written in the three languages of Ancient Egyptian hieroglyphs, demotic Egyptian and Greek. The Coptic language is now used only for liturgical purposes but it is the closest we can get to the demotic Egyptian spoken and written by the people of ancient Egypt. Indeed because of the rarity of intermarriage, the Copts see themselves as the true descendants of the ancient Egyptians and emphasise their high cheek-bones and almond-shaped eye appearances which are striking in the stunning Portraits of the Fayoum. In reality, though, Copts are distinguishable mainly by their Christian or ancient Egyptian names: Mary, George, Anthony or Ramses, Isis, Ptolemy etc, although more recently some have been given non-biblical names, eg Nasser.

    I became aware of them at school where my class always had a smattering of Sikas, Lozas, Ghalis and Wissa Wassefs (typical Coptic surnames) usually from large wealthy land-owning families from the Said in southern Egypt. I got to know them a good deal better through my close and continuing contact with the wonderful Loza family practically all of whom are psychiatrists and owners of the large, most prestigious private psychiatric hospital in the Middle East - the Behman Hospital in the Cairo suburb of Helwan. Fathy Loza was a few years ahead of me at Victoria College but I had never met him until our paths crossed at a World Congress of Psychiatry in Hawaii in the 1970's when he generously excused me for putting my foot in it. Seeing Ahmed Okasha, another Egyptian psychiatrist at a cocktail party, I said to him "I hear that one of Dr Behman's daughters, Francine, has married a Saidi" (a somewhat derogatory term for someone from the south). He turned to someone behind him and introduced me saying: "This is Dr Fathy Loza, the Saidi husband of Francine". We immediately liked one another and I rapidly became a friend of the family meeting his charming and very clued-up wife Francine – always a mine of information on the literary, artistic and social scene of Cairo and a generous hostess. I later got to know their older son, Nasser, also a psychiatrist, who spent many years at the Maudsley Hospital as an overseas student and is now a very big wheel in national and international psychiatry. In Egypt, he was recently based in the Ministry of Health as Director of Mental Health Services (he has recently resigned). Amongst other things he has been responsible for shepherding a new Mental Health Act through the Egyptian Parliament with the support of ex-President Mubarak.

With Francine and a bus load of Copts, I once had the opportunity of visiting the remarkable monasteries of Wadi Natrun which play a crucial role in the election of the Coptic Pope. They are staffed by monks the majority of whom have had previous careers in other professions and are busy with experimental agriculture and ecology. She also later took me to see the beautifully restored St Anthony and St Paul monasteries near the diving centre of Hurghada on the Red Sea. Although largely a religious designation, the term Copt has assumed a cultural dimension. For instance, some have converted to other branches of Christianity but continue to consider themselves and are seen by others as Copts. They are, undoubtedly, the subject of some persecution and discrimination which occasionally flares up into violence but usually remains at the bureaucratic level. For instance, Boutros Boutros Ghaly - one time Secretary General of the United Nations - was never appointed Foreign Secretary. Although directing Egyptian foreign policy for years, he remained a Minister of State. It is also impossible for a Copt to hold a senior academic position. On the other hand, no obstacles are put in the way of their business activities, often carried out in association with close friends or relatives of successive presidents. One of the richest families in Egypt are the Sawiris. They are Copts who were also close to ex-President Mubarak, but are now some of the leading figures in the democratic opposition. They own the massive Orascom conglomerate in which one brother is in building, one in telecommunications and one in tourism. At the other end of the social ladder, some of the poorest people in Cairo are also Copts. These include the notorious 'zabaleen' (garbage collectors) who lived in a slum in the Moqattam Hills and depended on thousands of pigs to consume the garbage they collected. One recent winter there was a massive slaughter of pigs carried out on the pretext that this was necessary to prevent swine 'flu. It had a devastating effect on the finances of the garbage collectors who have now been relocated in another, more distant part of the city. Coptic families have traditionally occupied important parts of the neighbourhoods of Shubrah and 'Old Cairo'.

Any visit to Cairo, as distinct from that to the ancient city of Memphis should include an early foray into 'Old Cairo' around the station of Mari Girguis on the Sadat-Helwan Metro line. When Amr ibn el Ghas took over and Islamised Egypt, he literally pitched his tents (fustat) in the area, later known as Fustat. There are, however, other suggested derivations of the word 'Fustat', eg from the Byzantine Greek 'phosseton', meaning 'entrenchment' or the Latin 'fossaton' which predates the Arab invasion of 642.

Such a visit is really one to a largely Coptic part of the city with the Coptic Museum, the Churches of El Mughlaqa, St Georges, St Sergius and St Barbara, as well as the Greek orthodox church of St Georges. There is also a bonus in the shape of the synagogue of Ben Ezra which may once have been the church of St Michael sold by the Copts to the Jewish community in order to pay the taxes imposed by Ibn Tulun. It is thought to be the oldest synagogue in the Middle East, if not the world. The most important relics of Amr are to be seen in the Coptic Museum - the best organised, quietest and most enjoyable museum in Cairo - far from the hassling touts.

I took the Metro from Sadat station in the Midan al Tahrir to Mari Girguis. Tickets cost LE1 (about 15p) for all journeys. There are now several new lines and the network will eventually extend to the Pyramids of Giza. The system is a good deal cleaner than the London tube but trains are crowded even in the middle of the day. I was impressed and humbled by the alacrity with which there was nearly always someone who gave me their seat without any need for the expression of 'grey power' required in London where I usually ask for one of the seats reserved for 'people less able to stand'. On the rare occasions when no one offered me their seat there was usually a bearded fundamentalist who issued a firm order to do so.

Arriving at Mari Girguis, I saw the looming dome of the Greek church of St Georges close to the recently restored Coptic museum - two large local houses with attractive musharabiahs (wooden fretwork screens) set in a pleasant modified French-style garden. As cameras were not allowed, I carried two and handed in one as I wished to photograph the exterior and parts of the garden which would not be affected by the flash. Although I was taking the law in my own hands, I saw no harm in this as I did not use the camera indoors and therefore caused no harm to any of the delicate displays. The chronological tour starts with some non-Coptic items related to Amr Ibn al Ghas, the Arab invader. I did the rounds of the practically deserted rooms which allowed for quiet contemplation – a luxury in this noisy city.

On leaving the museum, I collected my camera and made for the church of St Mary, almost invariably known locally as El Mughllaqa (the hanging one) on account of the fact that it literally hangs over an old fortress which became redundant. Although it claims an origin to the 4th century, this is disputed as it is difficult to see how this would be consistent with the present structure which is built on pre-existing Arab walls. Be that as it may, the sight was impressive in spite of the gaudy decorations put up for the Coptic Christmas. The succession of smaller local churches of St George, St Sergius and St Barbara are worth seeing as is the local cemetery. On the way, I found an arrow pointing to the synagogue of Ben Ezra but it was past 4pm, when the synagogue closes. I left Ben Ezra for the next day which I earmarked for 'Jewish Cairo'.

## Chapter 6

# JEWISH CAIRO, BEN EZRA, ADLY AND MAIMONIDES SYNAGOGUES

*T*he next morning I had a hearty breakfast at my hotel. After much effort, I managed to obtain whole uncrushed 'foul medames' (fava beans) with appropriate side dishes. On all previous days the beans laid out in the buffet came in the crushed and pounded form (foul mafroum), whereas I greatly prefer the uncrushed form (foul asli). I had to appeal to the manager for this in order to obtain decent Turkish coffee rather than the usual Nescafe on offer. I felt a great sense of achievement and set out once again for Mari Girguis and the Ben Ezra Synagogue.

This is said to be the oldest synagogue in the Middle East. It is surrounded by Coptic churches and one practically has to go though St Sergius to get to it. After starting life as a synagogue, it went through another incarnation when it was it was said to have been the church of St Michael and was sold by the Copts in order to pay for the taxes imposed by Ibn Tulun, so that it went through a number of transformations: synagogue, church then synagogue again.

In 1896 two remarkable Scottish twins Agnes Lewis and Margaret Gibson came across some manuscripts which ultimately led to a huge cache of documents in what is known as the Ben Ezra(or Cairo) Geniza. In Jewish law, any text mentioning God is sacred and is kept in a special part of the synagogue. Since no distinction was made between religious and non-religious texts either through expediency or illiteracy, some 200,000 sheets were found giving illuminating views of life in medieval Cairo. There is, for instance, a letter from Maimonides' brother, a trader, to the great man himself, physician to Saladin and eminent scholar revered by the Jewish community of Cairo. There is also a judgment by Maimonides in a dispute between a 'mowel' (circumciser) and a doctor who was taking business away from him .there is also some correspondence between Maimonides and his brother who was trading in India The bulk of it dealt with largely mundane business matters. The two ladies acquired some fragments and showed them Dr Solomon Schechter, the expert in Hebraic studies at Cambridge University. Schechter was naturally excited and made for Cairo where discovered the wealth of the Geniza and arranged for the transfer of 140,000 documents from the Ben Ezra synagogue to Cambridge University Library as a gift from the Jewish community of Cairo to Cambridge University where the bulk of the documents is now kept, though some are in Israel and others in the US. A recently built small building between Ben Ezra and the Coptic cemetery behind it now accommodates facsimiles of many of the most important Geniza texts as well as panels outlining the history of Jews of the locality. As the door was open and unattended, I walked in but an official soon arrived to drag me out to the sound of Mamnou'. I entered later.

When I first saw the partly restored Ben Ezra Synagogue in 1981, it consisted of one small room betraying the structure of the previous basilica and containing limited material. It has now been vastly expanded and restored. The walls and are covered in wooden panelling and musharabiah (Arabic fretwork). It is the only synagogue I saw which had a substantial number of visitors. When I tried to photograph inside it, a lady wearing a 'hejab' gave me a cheerful "Mamnou'" but led me to understand that if I made a donation, permission to photograph could be granted. As the sum involved seemed substantial, I demurred and relied instead on the poor quality postcards on sale at the desk. The lady holding the fort was clearly not Jewish but was, nevertheless, a mine of information about other synagogues in the City. "'Always take your passport", she warned.

After a brief saunter through the nearby Coptic cemetery, I made my way back to the station, passed underneath a bridge to the other side and then made my way towards the Nile knowing that there was a sort water-taxi which would take me back to the Maspero Corniche opposite the monstrously ugly Ramses Hilton. I found that I was in luck and the boat was due to leave. I paid my LE1 (15pence) for a ticket and got a delightful 45-minute boat trip past Rodah Island with its Nilometer (a remarkable piece of Mamluk technology employed to measure the height of the Nile during the annual floods) and the Museum devoted to the great singer Om Kalthoum, on to Giza on the other bank, and finally reached my central Cairo destination feeling rather hungry. In a small alley by the ugly concrete Ramses Hilton, I found a choice of local food including some delicious fresh taameya (falafel) served up by a joint called 'Falamina', recommended to me by the captain of the boat. Having wolfed down a sandwich of these inside the inimitable ghesh baladi (a whole-meal pitta with a gritty feel due to fragments of millet in with the flour), I felt ready for a visit of the main Cairo synagogue on Adly Street. Its real name is Shaar Hashamayin (The Gates of Heaven) but it is variously known as the Adly (after the name of the street where it is situated) Synagogue or the Ismaileya (the area of Cairo where it stands) Synagogue.

The Shaar Hashamayin is the principal synagogue of Cairo. It is where my parents were married and where I did my Barmitva (Jewish Confirmation). Built in 1905 in 'Egyptomania' style, it has two large staircases one leading to a central entrance, the other to the women's gallery. It was restored in 1980 after the Camp David accords and is in excellent condition. It is now surrounded by a metal barricade and is heavily guarded by the tourist police. I arrived and after an unconvincing Mamnou' showed my passport to the guard at the side-gate who took me to his boss in a small office on the right and was soon introduced to what turned out to be the librarian of the synagogue. I took him at first to be the shamash (caretaker) and was surprised by his youth. He was a young man aged 33 was called Hani Salama. He made it clear that there were no restrictions on photography but I desisted as I had taken many on a previous visit. Born and bred in Cairo, he had studied Hebrew at Cairo University. I wrongly took him to be Jewish and he did not correct me. He told me that there were now only 200 Jews in the city most of them elderly and infirm, and that the community was led by the formidable Carmen Weinstein who had been in dispute with various people in the Egyptian Jewish Diaspora. They wished to remove originals of certain documents eg 'kotubas (marriage contracts) etc, and move them to what they considered to be a safer place outside Egypt while she has fiercely defended them as part of Egypt's heritage to be left where they belonged.

Hani told me that services were held every Friday evening and Saturday mornings (a fabrication or out-and-out lie) but that there were occasions when it was difficult to make up a minian(a quorum of ten men as required by Jewish law.) Occasionally, they had to drag in some tourists or visiting diplomats to make up the numbers. On the other hand, the suburban Maadi synagogue which is close to the Israeli Embassy is in much more frequent use with embassy staff making up the numbers. The locals in Maadi complain that the presence of the Israeli Ambassador's house and the synagogue mean that, for security purposes, several Maadi streets around have had to be permanently blocked.

Hani took me on a tour of the synagogue which had not changed materially since visits in the 1980's and 1990's. The exception being the conversion of a community hall to an impressive library opened in the presence of President Mubarak in 1997.

This contains valuable manuscripts some dating 500 years back and written either in Judeo-Spanish or Judeo-Arabic, ie either using Hebrew letters to write Arabic or Arabic letters to write Hebrew. He confirmed to me that the Rab Moshe synagogue celebrating Maimonides was being restored. It would reopen later in the next year (2010). I later heard that Hani was the librarian and was not Jewish but sometimes pretended to tourists that he was. He later got into trouble and was sacked when his pretence of being Jewish went beyond what was acceptable when he began to 'invite' Jewish tourists to mock Fridays (Shabat) or other ceremonies and used this to extract money from them.

No description of the synagogues of Egypt can omit that of Rab Moshe (Maimonides) in the ghetto (Haret el Yahoud). When I first revisited it was closed for extensive restoration. It had always held a special place for the Jewish community of Cairo. This is partly because of the towering stature of Moses Maimonides as probably the most important character in Sephardi history and partly because of the supposed near-miraculous effect of a night spent there either by one who is ill or by a relative.

Moses Maimonides was born in 1135 on the eve of Passover in Cordoba, a city where he is now celebrated by numerous statues and a street named after him in the Juderia (Jewish Quarter). When I was last in Cordoba some years ago lecturing about Alzheimer's disease to a group of Spanish psychiatrists, I was presented with a large rusty key said to be one which opened the Juderia (Jewish Quarter). I also received numerous apologies for the nasty treatment received there by my ancestors. Maimonides lived and worked in this city where he was a physician, a theologian a philosopher, translator and adaptor of the writings of Aristotle from Greek into Arabic before their reappearance in Latin in which form they spread to the rest of the world. When things started to become difficult for the Jews, he went to Morocco where he converted to Islam and thence to Cairo where he reverted to Judaism and was made welcome becoming personal physician to Salah el Din el Ayubi (Saladin) founder of the Ayubic dynasty. His synagogue is located in the Jewish quarter where it previously assumed an important role in local Jewish life. It was here that he wrote his most well-known work, 'The Guide to the Perplexed', written in Arabic with Hebrew letters. He died in 1204 and is buried in Tiberias, now in Israel.

His synagogue is surprisingly small. It is rectangular, about 20 by 10 metres, and has a facade with a semicircular entrance. The door is closed by two iron gates and above the entrance there is a marble slab in the shape of an open book on which are written the Ten Commandments. It was declared a national monument in 1986. It was badly damaged in the earthquake of 1992. The restorations which were currently being carried out as part of the works on Fatimid Cairo were only recently completed.

As I left, I remarked to myself that as an atheist I had done more than my duty by the synagogues.

## Chapter 7

# THE RESTORATION OF THE MAIMONIDES SYNAGOGUE

On one of my earlier trips, I had tried to visit this important 13th century synagogue which was in the heart of the Jewish Quarter. I was unable to do so as it was under intense restoration. On this second occasion, I heard that the restorations were nearing completion. I 'phoned up Carmen Weinstein, Head of the Jewish Community and she said: "You can't see it unless you make a donation of several thousand pounds sterling to the community". Not being sure whether she was serious or was joking, I said: "I am a poor pensioner and can't afford this kind of money". "You must have made a lot of money in your day", she replied. She nevertheless invited me to tea in Maadi on a day which had, anyway, set aside to go and see my friend Francine who lived round the corner.

I had a bit of difficulty finding her, as her flat was being redone and she was occupying a rough piece of land adjoining the Maadi Synagogue. She had found this full of rubbish and had cleaned it out and turned it into a fairly attractive garden and was living in a shack in this garden. We had an amiable conversation about the arrangements for the re-opening of the Synagogue and the programme of events around it. She explained that the Jewish Community was hard up and that she had to try to raise funds for the upkeep and for the opening event. I promised to do all I could to obtain some sponsorship when I got back to London. We discussed the life of Maimonides, his work as a physician to Salah el Din el Ayubi (Saladin) and the finding of letters from his brother in the Cairo Geniza. She told me of an anecdote about how Maimonides obtained his medical post. The Sultan had a large boil on his bottom. He was recommended to consult a clever Jewish doctor. When Maimonides arrived, Saladin asked him "Will it take long?" "Take your clothes off and bend down please, Your Honour". He gave a big slap to the healthy buttock while he lanced the boil on the other. "It's done". That 'made his day' and his reputation.

While we were talking we were joined by Samir Rafaat who had been helping her to keep the Bassatine News Website( a site for and about the Jewish Community) up-to-date (it had been pirated). He is a journalist who is a mine of information about Cairo and who has written several books on the city – notably one on the history of Maadi. We chatted about this and that and firmed up the arrangements for the opening of the synagogue. I left for Francine's house pleased to have established a good relationship with Carmen.

On my return to the UK, I went about trying to raise funds. My first approach was to Lord Janner, as Carmen told me he had offered to help. I rang the House of Lords and was told he would ring me back. When he did so, he told me that I had interrupted his lunch and it was clear that he had no intention of helping. Subsequent approaches to Professor Nasser Khalili, founder of the Maimonides Centre, and to Sir Ronald Cohen, who was born in Cairo, were successful in that each offered to make a contribution. Sir Ronald wrote from Israel to ask for a photograph of the restored synagogue, if possible.

In an exchange of emails with Carmen Weinstein, I discovered that the reopening of the restored synagogue was fixed for

## The restoration of the Maimonides Synagogue

the 7th March 2010. It was to be followed by two days of visits of other synagogues and of the Bassatine Jewish Cemetery. I was invited to these events and my daughter, Simone, and her husband, Ayhan, decided to join me for the five days I had set aside for this third trip. Ayhan, though born in Cairo, had not been back for nearly 20 years and looked forwards to seeing his uncle Yehia and his cousins. These few days turned out to be the most action-packed, incident-prone, exciting, moving and infuriating days I have ever experienced in the city of my birth.

I will try and tease out some of the strands involved in this complex and action-packed trip here I will deal largely with events during and around the reopening of the Maimonides Synagogue. (Fig9) We were taken to the Mousky area by minibus. On the bus, I came across a selection of Jews who had previously lived in Cairo or Alexandria and were now in France, Switzerland, Canada or the USA. As we approached the Synagogue, it became clear that a state of the highest security had been declared. The streets around were closed and people who lived nearby had been instructed not to open their windows. We were all frisked by the security staff and asked to show our passports. On entering the synagogue and the attached Yeshiva (School), I was bowled over by the excellent standard of the restoration achieved by the Department of Antiquities. It had perhaps been somewhat over restored but the craftsmanship was excellent.

When I had last seen the place, it had no roof, was flooded and was generally in a pitiful state. It has been subtly reconstructed, a new roof put in place and the decorations were back to what records indicate to be their original form. Special attention had been paid to the 12th century Yeshiva where Maimonides had studied and taught and where supposed 'medical miracle cures' had taken place much later. I was reminded that Maimonides himself was a rationalist and that he had no truck with supposed 'miracles', a point which he tried to drum into his students.

The audience consisted of around 150 – 200 people - some local Jews, a few Muslims who were part of the organisation, a number of ex-Egyptian Jews (more from Alexandria than from Cairo), a few US and Canadian Jews with no previous contact with Egypt, a couple of Israeli scholars, the present and past Israeli Ambassadors, the US Ambassador and a representative of the Spanish Ministry of Culture and the Casa Sefarad (a centre for the study of the Sephardi past in Spain). Also very prominent and sticking out like a sore thumb were 11 bearded and cheerful 'Chabad' rabbis clad in their traditional Hassidic black hats and coats. Although really out of place, they added a certain gaiety and swing to the occasion with their violins, accordions, etc, and a bottle of vodka.

After the formal speeches, the rabbis passed round the bottle of vodka, taking occasional swigs at it and started to dance traditional Ashkenazi dances to the sound of Hebrew and Yiddish tunes. Although I missed the previously advertised Sephardi music, I was drawn to their circle and danced with them together with a couple of the ambassadors. The audience clearly enjoyed this. It should be said that this single bottle of vodka was used by Zahi Haws in particular as an excuse for the cancellation of a later official ceremony at the synagogue which was due to occur a week later Feeling that Egypt had not been sufficiently remembered in all this, I took the microphone and sang 'Taalili Ya Bata' (Come to me my d duck), an old Egyptian song I remembered from my youth. This received a 'mixed reception' with some obviously feeling that it was inappropriate in a synagogue while others like Yousry (Carmen's companion) urging me to substitute 'Taalili ya Carmen' (Come to me Carmen) for the original words.

While mixing with the assembled company, I had the occasion of meeting a number of extremely interesting people. Yves Fedida from Alexandria and Paris (of the Nabi Daniel Association) who had a lot to do with the restoration by his goading of the Egyptian authorities, Lucette Lagnado (of The Wall Street Journal) and author of the acclaimed 'Man in the White Sharkskin Suit'). Robert Naggar from Alexandria and Geneva, with whom I struck an immediate friendship, and the extremely learned Israeli scholar, Yoram Meital.

In the afternoon, we were transported to the central Cairo Gates of Heaven Synagogue (Char Ha Chamayim or

## The restoration of the Maimonides Synagogue

Adly Street). The high security was even more evident and understandably so as a week earlier a stray amateur 'terrorist' had attsempted to throw a suit case full of explosives at the Synagogue from a hotel across the road. The suit case fell on the pavement outside the hotel where it exploded fortunately causing no injury to life or property. The man ran off and was apprehended by the police a few days later. His photograph in the local papers suggested that he had been given pretty rough treatment. . Doubts have been expressed about his sanity but at the time of writing nothing more is known about the man or his motives.

The Synagogue itself was decked out as for a feast day and after a tour of the premises there were a series of lectures inter alia by an Israeli Hebrew scholar about the so-called 'miracle cures' that had occurred in the Rambam (Maimonides) Yeshiva and which he had heard about from ex-Egyptian Jews in Israel. At this stage, I began to feel increasingly uncomfortable both by the high profile played by Israelis as distinct from ex locals and by the unbalanced account of the 'miracles' with the prospect of turning the Yeshiva into a sort of Jewish Lourdes. I asked whether the lecture was to be followed by questions and was informed by Carmen that I was free to comment if I felt like it. I took to the podium and while, congratulating the speaker on his faith, I reminded both him and the audience that Maimonides himself did not believe in miracles and were he alive, he would probably ask for a 'double blind' trial. I remarked to the audience that faith had both positive and negative aspects and that the Middle East had suffered from exaggerated and misplaced faith. This was received very badly by the audience many of whom expressed their disgust to me. One lady told my daughter that she felt like hitting me. Even the sceptical Bob Naggar told me that, though he agreed with what I said, he thought it was inappropriate to say it in a synagogue. I replied that we were to spend three days in synagogues and that there would not be any other occasion to raise this matter. In any case, the Synagogue was not being used for religious purposes but was, in fact, functioning as a lecture theatre. Having made myself unpopular, I decided that I should, henceforth, watch my tongue and apply a strict 'Mamnou'' on my remarks.

An early dinner was served under a colourful marquee tent set out in the courtyard of the synagogue. We sat at a table with three Jewish ladies who were still living in Egypt. Mrs Sylvera, near me, worked as a lawyer in the field of intellectual property and she described what life was like for the remaining 30 Jewish women who remained in Egypt. She also told me that her father, who had been a communist and Egyptian nationalist, had refused to leave Egypt in the massive exodus but had been arrested and remained in prison for some time on no specific charge.

In the self-service area a young Israeli wearing a kippa (skull-cap) who had previously expressed revulsion at Arabic being spoken in a synagogue, complained that the food was not fully kosher. I explained to him that with no rabbis and certainly no kosher butchers in Cairo, it would have been impossible to provide him with what he wanted. Why had he come to Cairo anyway if he was so uncomfortable and unhappy about everything? We were witnessing something extraordinary with a large number of lay and religious Jews in the middle of Muslim Cairo. To me that was the miracle. I failed to convince him.

# Chapter 8

# THE KARAITE SYNAGOGUE OF ABBASEYA AND THE BASSATINE JEWISH CEMETERY

The Karaites are a Jewish sect who only accept the writings of the Torah (Old Testament) and reject all subsequent oral traditions including the Talmud. They probably arose in Baghdad in the 7$^{th}$ century. They are not accepted by the official Jewish organisations. Cairo always had a certain number of Karaites some of whom I remember as friends of my parents. Many were jewellers and they usually lived in the area of Heliopolis and Abbaseya, where they had a number of synagogues. I always thought of them as somewhat mysterious though all I knew about them was that, instead of attaching the tefelim (philactories) to their forehead, they hung them from a nail in the wall literally 'in front of the eyes' as prescribed. I did not have any friends in that community myself so that they remained a bit of a mystery.

When a group of us attending the re-dedication of Maimonides' Synagogue came to Cairo, a small programme was prepared. This included a visit to a Karaite Synagogue. Although we were told that there was only one Karaite left in Cairo, we were taken to one of the restored synagogues - that of Moussa el Dere. This was fortunate for me as I learnt a little bit more about them: for instance, the fact that like Muslims they remove their shoes in places of worship, ie the wearing of shoes in the synagogue is strictly Mamnou'. Apart from a talk about them and a poem written by a Karaite writer, it gave us more of a chance to mix and to get to know one another. I was delighted to meet Yoram-Meital from Israel who is an expert on the Jews of Egypt and their monuments and, even more so, by the fact that he was put on this path by Shimon Shamir, who was one of the first Israeli ambassadors to Egypt and whom I had had the pleasure of meeting for dinner in Cairo, soon after the Israeli-Egyptian accords. Yoram, like Shimon, spoke impeccable Arabic including the colloquial Egyptian form. He seemed to have a real understanding of and sympathy with Egyptian society today.

After this visit we were taken to the Bassatine Jewish cemetery which has been a subject of some controversy. The accounts I had previously read mentioned desecration of tombs and other horrors. The place is certainly eerie and ill-kept, particularly compared with the Jewish cemeteries of Alexandria. A large motorway has been built nearby and the cemetery, like many in Cairo, was previously occupied by poor families with no homes. Most of the marble slabs covering the tombs were missing and some names had been written in black paint on the sides of some tombs. Some say that the slabs were stolen either by those who previously lived in the cemetery or by those who had built the motorway. It is difficult to call this desecration, as to me to me it assumes deliberate damage, opening of tombs and the writing of offensive graffiti which we have seen in Europe. None of this was to be seen. I was even fortunate and moved to find the tomb of my maternal grandfather, Rafoul Bigio, who died in 1944. It was intact though naturally covered in dust. The two simple policemen on duty helped me to wash it and to photograph it. One of them even said: "You must be a good man as Allah has preserved your grandfather's tomb and led you to it". I had come across it by chance and the experience brought tears to my eyes. My memory of grandfather was hazy but I did remember him as officiating at the large Passover meals which my grandmother had cooked. I have subsequently been surprised to find him on the family tree of another ex-Egyptian Jew, Alec Nacamuli, who came from Alexandria but had Cairo connections. Also amusingly enough 'Khawaga Bigio' has become a character in sketches on Cairo radio, where he is portrayed as a foreigner who is usually swindled by the canny locals. There were times in Cairo when I felt like a 'Khawaga Bigio'.

# Chapter 9

# SUNDAY LUNCH IN MAADI

My friend, Francine, has Sunday lunch with her children, grandchildren and their friends every week in the attractive Loza house in Maadi. I had an invitation for the next Sunday. "We eat late", she said. "So come about 2pm or even 2.30pm". They live in the smart suburb of Maadi which I knew well. My parents used to play bowls at the Maadi Sporting Club and I learnt to swim in its pool, and to play tennis on its clay courts. My school, Victoria College, was also situated there during my last two years leading up to my 'A level' examinations.

The word Maadi means 'ferries' in Arabic (from the fact that goods had to be carried over the flooded Nile). It is a very attractive suburb, planned and designed from scratch in a manner which was quite exceptional for Egypt in those days. A number of far-sighted Jewish bankers were responsible for its planning and construction. In 1888, the three firms of Jacob Moise Cattaui Fils et Cie, Menasche Fils et Cie and Suares Freres et Cie, created a consortium which obtained from the then ruler of Egypt, Khedive Tewfik, a concession to build, operate and manage a railway line running along the Nile from Cairo to the small town of Helwan, south of the capital. In the next few years, they bought a considerable amount of previously agricultural land lying to the west of the proposed train line. In this they were later joined by the sharp-operator cousins, Victor and Nessim Mosseri', who quickly bought up land on both sides of the new line. The history of this venture has been told magnificently by the scholarly and much underestimated journalist, Samir Rafaat, in 'Maadi 1904-1962 – Society and History of a Cairo suburb'. Rafaat's other book 'Cairo-The Glory years' is another admirable text on the Architecture of the Cairo of the 'Belle Epoque'

As my invitation was basically for the afternoon, I had a morning in which to occupy myself usefully. I decided to spend a few hours in the Khan Khalili Bazaar to buy a few presents. The bazaar is in the Fatimid part of the City. I plunged into its depths passing by the famous Cafe Fishawi which used to be a favourite haunt of the novelist and Nobel prize-winner, Naguib Mahfouz, before the attempt on his life. I got 'Hey ministered' on the way and gave my usual reply. After a quick look at the tourist tat my eye fell on a series of tarbouches (Egyptian form of fez which are slightly taller) of different sizes. I decided to get a couple of small ones for my grandchildren and a much bigger one for my half-Egyptian son-in-law, Ayhan. Although I quickly looked away with a show of detached indifference, I was too late. "You want a tarbouche, ya bey. They are very good quality, pure wool. I make a special price for you LE30". "You must be joking". I replied. "You should be giving them away. Nobody wears a tarbouche these days. They are "Mamnou". They were abolished by Gamal Abd el Nasser". "LE25 specially for you because you speak Arabic". "I am feeling generous but don't really want one. I will give you LE10 for an adult one". "Impossible, I would be losing money". "OK look, I will give you LE20 for one adult and two children's sizes". He looked dubious. I walked away but after a minute he came running after me. "OK. I will let you have them for LE20 as you are my first client of the day. Having practised my bargaining skills, which had laid dormant for years, I made for the Bab el Zuweila - the most attractive and

## Sunday Lunch in Maadi

elaborate of the Fatimid gates of Cairo. It is sometimes called Bab el Metwalli. On the way, I applied my talents in buying some 'bolghas' ( pointed yellow leather slippers). As time was pressing and I needed to make my way to the station for the Maadi Metro, I added my aching body to the grapevines hugging the appropriate bus and got off not far from the station and long before I needed to pay the conductor. On the short walk to the station, I passed by some places selling 'Koshari' and 'fatayer', both very common fellah dishes which were seldom seen in Cairo in my day but have become common since the village has invaded the City. I desisted, having in mind the large meal which awaited in Maadi. Taking the Metro I arrived at about 2pm at Maadi station. "Too early, I thought". So I looked round the smart Maadi shops and at 2.30pm took a short taxi ride to my host only to find that I was still too early. There was no one around. I sat with a Stella beer and some pistachios reading some of the magazines which were lying around. Soon Francine appeared and said she did not think we would be lunching until 4pm but to keep me occupied, I could do her son Nasser a favour and give him a second opinion on a local patient. The chauffeur took me round to their house which was, in fact, within walking distance and took longer to get to by car as the road, which passes by the Israeli Ambassador's house, was blocked to cars for security purposes. I stayed with the patient till 4pm feeling increasingly hungry and regretting that I had not eaten a portion of Koshari earlier on.

When I got back, some people had arrived and we sat down to a sumptuous meal of lentil soup, stuffed cabbages and vine leaves together with some delicious chicken and lamb. Unlike in other Egyptian households, this is very much a' take it or leave it affair' without the hostess urging you to have more of this or that. The meal ended with Om Ali (a traditional Egyptian trifle-type desert) and other more European deserts. Over Turkish coffee, I chatted to Khaled, the only non-psychiatrist in the family who has just returned from a marina in Greece where his yacht was moored. A lean, sun-tanned figure, he was pretty laid-back about most things .He must be one of the most eligible bachelors in Cairo. He took a relaxed view of Egypt's political problems and was clearly determined to go on enjoying his sailing ,swimming and other aquatic activities. He now lives in Gouna near Hurgada on the Red Sea where he owns a successful bar and is clearly unfazed by the islamist victory in the last elections. After our conversation I got the chauffeur to drive me to the Metro station taking me back to town.

## Chapter 10

# A PSYCHIATRIST AGAIN?

When visiting Cairo 'officially' in the past, I have occasionally been asked to give an opinion on a patient. It is something that I have usually resisted but it is not always easy to do so without getting into deep waters. These encounters have invariably been very interesting in one way or another. They are difficult to write about without breaking an implied confidence except, of course, when the person concerned has long been dead. Since they shed light on aspects of Egyptian life I will give an example or two while disguising the identity of the patient where necessary.

On one occasion many years ago I was asked to see Ismail Fahmy, an ex-foreign minister who was thought to be suffering from Alzheimer's disease. I went to see him in his large flat overlooking the Nile and was met by a distinguished looking elderly gentleman who spoke very interestingly of his life and diplomatic career. He produced illuminating portraits of the key actors on the world stage: Nixon, Carter, Kissinger, Brezhnev and, especially, Sadat. He explained that he had always been in favour of a negotiated peace with Israel but believed that this should be prepared by wide consultations within and outside Egypt. He thoroughly disapproved of the way Sadat had impulsively travelled to Jerusalem and settled the matter in bilateral negotiations which isolated Egypt though, of course, obtaining the return of captured Sinai. Fahmy considered this as an empty gesture which postponed a comprehensive peace in the Middle East for many decades. This disagreement with his President had led to his resignation which Sadat told him he accepted with great sadness. He thought that Sadat's advisors had pressed him for an arrest and charge of treason. but he believed that Sadat had resisted this suggestion and understood Fahmy's position as a traditional diplomat.

We spoke of his life since his resignation. It seemed that he got out of bed late, spent most of his day pottering around at home but occasionally went out for a short walk in the nearby Gezira Club. He ceased to read or to have any social life. Quite rightly, he considered his life to be empty. Although discussion with his relatives indicated occasional absent- mindedness, there was nothing really indicative of Alzheimer's disease. He struck me as a very depressed man who had exchanged a busy, stimulating life with one of fickle idleness and lack of interest and who should be treated for depression. As I left he gave me a signed copy of his book 'Negotiating for Peace in the Middle East'. Over the years I heard of his occasional brief improvement but his condition remained basically unchanged with ups and downs until his death in 1997.

During my more recent trip my 'consultation' occurred while waiting for Sunday lunch at Francine's in Maadi. The patient was said to have been depressed since his son had been involved in a major car accident. Fortunately, the son had escaped relatively unharmed but his father had nevertheless become very concerned about the possible long-term effects. I went to see him at his home and was able to speak to his wife. He was retired academic aged 75. It became clear that his depression had started a couple of years before the son's accident. The problem which concerned me most was the fact that he was being treated by a life-long friend and that the treatment was being conducted on the telephone. Doses of different medication had been prescribed, sometimes in inappropriate doses which had, at least once, produced serious side-effects. Furthermore, the patient had not had a full physical examination although he showed some signs which might indicate early Parkinson's disease. I explained to him and his wife that I thought that the current medical arrangements were not satisfactory and that he should seek treatment from someone, who was not a close friend, who would be able to assess his case by face-to-face consultation, and after a full physical examination. While the wife was fully in agreement with this, the patient had doubts and thought that his friend might be offended if he sought treatment elsewhere. I explained that the use of a second opinion was common in medicine and did not cast any doubts about the competence of the original doctor. It looked, at first, as though he might see things my way but, by the time I left, he had already changed his mind. He did eventually accept that he should see a neurologist to explore the possibility of early Parkinson's disease and find an alternative arrangement for treatment. When I heard from him last, it seemed that he had improved.

The examples I have given illustrate the relative informality of professional relationships in Cairo. Medical treatment, at least amongst the middle classes, is often organised through personal contacts and is far less regulated than in Europe. Although this is often beneficial it does occasionally lead to difficulties which can militate against the most effective assessment and treatment of those concerned. However, it is easier to point to the disadvantages of a particular mode of operation than to put it right.

I felt better in returning to my tourist role.

# Chapter 11

# PHARAONIC CAIRO

To a large extent, ancient Egyptian Cairo consists of the Cairo Museum, the Pyramids and Sphinx of Giza together with the Solar Boat Museum, North and South Saqqara and the remains of Memphis, Abu Sir and the pyramids of Dahshur and Meidun. Most tourists, rushing through the city, limit themselves to the Cairo museum and the pyramids of Giza - a great pity as the Zoser funerary complex and the Stepped Pyramid of Saqqara, together with the Imhotep museum and the pyramids of Dahshur, are far more rewarding. Detailed consideration of these sites is beyond the scope of this book but I would like to describe some of my experiences at Saqqara – a real jewel worth a day's excursion. The development of the site and the pyramid of Zoser owe everything to a remarkable Frenchman called Jean-Phillipe Lauer who died recently at the age of 99. Some years ago, when he was still living on the site I was fortunate to meet him. He was a lean and grizzled old man, still full of energy and with little time to chat with the casual visitor. An architect by training (like Imhotep), he discovered the site in 1926 and never left it. He eventually built himself a simple house there and moved in with his family. He was worshiped by the local guards and workmen as he ate with them and treated them well.

On a more recent visit after his death, one of the guards, hearing me speak French, remembered Lauer - 'Allah yermamou' (God bless his soul) - and regretted that he was no longer there with them. "He was a real gentleman", he said. "He treated us like human beings unlike the young people now". He praised Lauer's work, that of Mariette and his French predecessors, and thought that perhaps Napoleon's brief invasion was worth it for what it brought Egypt. Other nearby guards chimed in with their praise for Lauer. They were particularly critical of modern Egyptian archaeologists.

On to the Giza Pyramids……..

I had not been to the Giza pyramids for donkey's years although, they are, of course, the main tourist attraction of Cairo and many myths are associated with them. In my youth, I used to drive my jeep to it and into the desert around it. My friends and I used to tease the caléches-drivers by calling them 'Abu Laban'. This infuriated them for reasons which were never clear to me. In fact, I have never been able to find the true meaning of this term which means 'father of milk'. I suspect that it hinted at masturbation though I am not sure, and as the term has ceased to be used, no one has been able to help me. These drivers often took couples who used to embrace affectionately in the back and sometimes 'went further'. The driver was also sometimes referred to as 'Chamaghangui' (candle holder or third man) which makes more sense. On previous visits, I had concentrated on the more rewarding pyramids at Saqqara and Daashour which are less thronged with visitors. On this occasion, I felt I could no longer avoid a visit to this all too familiar place. At breakfast, I met a Chinese young man (call me Alex for short) who was responsible for selling and inspecting video cameras for security purposes in the Maghreb and the Middle East. During a casual conversation, I had a devil of a job persuading him that Napoleon was not responsible for knocking the nose off the Sphinx. I explained to

## Pharaonic Cairo

him that the famous 'Battle of the Pyramids' had taken place a long way away in the suburb of Imbabah.

On leaving my hotel, I was hailed by taxi and negotiated with the driver a price for taking me to the Pyramids, the nearby Sphinx and the pharaonic boat, staying with me for a couple of hours, and taking me back into town. The journey was of course a familiar one past the University, the Zoo and the Mukhtar statue, 'The Birth of Egypt'.

On the way, we passed the dilapidated place which previously housed the 'Auberge des Pyramides' much used in the 1940s and 1950s by King Farouk and by the cosmopolitans classes of the city as a night club and casino. Two other memorable places on the way were the Art Centre of Ramses Wissa Wasef, where children are taught to weave the now much- prized carpets. These very attractive and much copied works were the rage in Paris a few years ago but much of the international interest in them has dwindled – a chance to acquire them as wall hangings or carpets. Andrea's Restaurant is the other landmark on the old road to the Giza Pyramids. It is a great place to enjoy typical Egyptian food much of it barbequed in the open air. There are now two Andreas on the way to the Pyramids - one for meat, poultry, stuffed vegetables, etc, and one for fish.

On to the sumptuous and historic Mena House Hotel, which has been lovingly restored and expanded. It is currently part of the Indian Oberoi chain which runs many hotels in Egypt always impeccably. I treated myself to a Turkish coffee and shisha (hubble-bubble) while reminiscing wildly about old times.

While queuing for the Pyramids entry ticket, I remarked to Ibn Mustapha (the taxi driver) that the difference between the entry for Egyptians and that for foreigners was enormous (LE2 versus LE60). He suggested that since I had a good accent, I should try and get a ticket as an Egyptian. The psychopath in me readily agreed and I tried my hand at this relatively innocent bit of fraud. Delighted at getting a local ticket, I presented it at the entrance but was told Mamnou' and asked to show an identity card forcing me to join the queue again for a LE60 ticket.

Once inside, I did not bother to visit the Pyramids which had not changed, but I went about trying to engage people in conversation which was my self-imposed brief. For once, I had great difficulties because the Egyptians were mainly dragomen chasing tourists for their custom and the foreigners were busy running away from a mysterious man who spoke their language. The problem was made worse by the fact that I did not carry a camera, for there is nothing more effective than a pointed camera to get people talking. I had limited success with a small group from Genoa, who had to be dissuaded from believing the 'New Age 'stories about the pyramids having been built by Martians. I had to soften the blow with admiring words on Ligurian cooking.

I cast a quick look at the 'Solar boat' meant to ferry the pharaoh to the other side in his after life. Following this rapid reminder of the important tourist sites, I got Ibn Mustapha to take me back into town where I got off at Kasr el Nil Bridge and ordered some stuffed pigeons in a restaurant by the Nile.

The Egyptian Museum is another of the key tourist sites of Cairo and the focus of much attention during the Tahrir Square demonstrations, when it was broken into in spite of the spirited defence put up by the demonstrators to defend it. An amateurish burglary resulted in the breakage of one of the display cases and the removal of ancient objects some of which have been returned. It was founded by the pioneer Egyptologist, Auguste Marriette, in 1858, who was later buried in the grounds. His statue graces the garden entrance. The Museum itself has always had a special place in my heart, partly because it stands near my birth-place in nearby Antikhana, now Basiouni Street, to which it is joined by Champollion Street and, partly because it stimulated an early interest in Egyptology. I always go and a pay a visit to Tut Ankh Amoun's mummy which now lies with only the face and feet showing. Although the Museum is enormous and crammed full of marvels, its full description does not have a place here except for the fact that on a recent visit, I was asked at the Ticket Office whether I was Egyptian or foreign ("Masry walla agnabi"). When I replied "Agnabi" (foreigner), the man at the ticket office explained "Lazem Masri" (Must be Egyptian), thus saving me the more expensive ticket. I was pumped up with pride at this compliment to my Arabic which stayed with me throughout my visit of the crowded building, due to be replaced by a new Museum within the next few years.

Having done my tourist bit, I set out on a culinary pursuit which had been on my mind for a while.

## Chapter 12

# THE SEARCH FOR A FAMOUS SOUP

From the moment of my arrival, I had been searching for a place where I could have classical molokheya made with rabbit stock. This is a very traditional, green, somewhat glutinous soup which goes back to the pharaonic age. In fact, the word itself is said by some to derive from 'malakeya' meaning 'royal' since leaves of were found in Pharaonic tombs. Odly enough, it has become a great favourite in Japan where it is put into saches and used as an infusion for medicinal purposes. The plant has green leaves, which look a bit like spinach leaves and the plant itself has a certain resemblance to cannabis. I believe that the English term for it is 'Jew's Mallow' though I have never heard it used. I cook it in London using the frozen leaves which produce an acceptable result but there is no real substitute for fresh leaves and rabbit stock with pieces of rabbit, and not too many bones if possible. On my second evening in Cairo while walking round the streets of Zamalek not far from the President Hotel in Taha Husein Street, I found a likely place.

It was dark and the waiters were watching the television. "Do you have molokheya?" I ask. "Yes. Of course". So I settled down to a perfectly decent one cooked with lamb. I had, however, to put up with watching the Ahli v Ismailia football match on TV. Ahli won 3-1. An OK evening but not exactly what I was after.

The next morning at breakfast I asked a waiter for the best place to have it. "The best molokheya in Cairo", he said emphatically, "is to be had at the 'El Brince' in Imbabah across the river". Imbabah has the reputation of being a hot-bed of fundamentalism and, at one time, constituted itself as an 'The Islamic Republic'. However, I am determined to go there that evening.

In the course of the day, I got a call from my friend, Nasser Loza, who had just returned from London and wanted to see me before I left. He said that he would be busy all day but was having dinner with his in-laws not far from my hotel. "What about a drink about 6pm in your area?" "I was planning to go to 'El Brince' in Inbabah for a molokheya", I .replied There was a deathly hush from the other end. Imbabah is not the sort of area where a gent like Nasser would go. "Imbabah is too far out of my way", came the reply at last. "Why don't you have it at AbuSid?" "I will have beer there while you eat". "OK, Abu Sid it is". I replied, knowing that this was at the opposite end of the price and smartness spectrum. I got ready for 6pm but there was no Nasser. Egyptians are not known for their punctuality, so I waited until 7.30pm and rang him. No reply. I decided to walk to the restaurant and to make the best of the evening.

On the way, I rang again and got hold of him. "Sorry I have been busy all day and missed you on the 'phone. I am about to leave. As I have explained Abu Sid is not 'Al Brince' It is an extremely smart, trendy restaurant hidden behind plush disguised doors but nevertheless serves authentic Egyptian food some of which cannot easily be found outside the home or at certain times of the year, eg Ashoura - a delicious desert usually only found during the feast of Ashoura. When I arrived I found that there were no free tables. I sat at the bar, where it is possible, to eat and I borrowed a mobile from a young man, who had just got engaged to an Egyptian girl currently living in

## The search for a famous soup

Brighton. We finally got Nasser who, when informed that there were no tables, said: "Don't worry. This is Egypt. They know me and will find me a table." In the meantime my food arrived including the much awaited molokheya - with rabbit. Nasser also turned up and was hailed with obsequious respect by the staff who were nevertheless unable to produce a table. He joined me at the bar at 9pm. We each knocked back some Stella beer while I tucked into my food. The molokheya was a bit of an anti-climax I am afraid. Too many bones, though the soup was excellent. Our conversation was interrupted by a few mobile calls and some medical school colleagues whom had not seen him for ages. He tried to explain to me the difficulties he was having in getting a new Mental Health Act through Parliament although the President had already signed it. A rear guard action was being mounted by a few prominent psychiatrists who objected to clauses making them subject to criticism if they made a serious mistake. The meal and drinks over, Nasser offered me a lift back to my hotel with his chauffeur. "I thought you were having dinner with your in-laws. It's 10pm". "You know how it is. This is Egypt. You can turn up at any time. Nobody minds." However he had an errand to complete on the way. He had some pungent cheese ('Munster' I think) he had bought in Paris during a brief crossing from London. He had got it for his hosts at dinner the next day but it was stinking out the car and he wanted to get rid of it. He delivered it to his hosts 'bawab' and the chauffeur took me back to my hotel. I decided that I could never stand the pace of living and working in Cairo even if there had been no other obstacles! When I told Nasser that I was including the incident in this book, his reply was that his father had taught him that only bored people turned up on time! I was certainly not bored by my next encounters at a famous cafe.

# Chapter 13

# THE CAFE RICHE AND OTHER CAFES

The Cafe Riche was a landmark in the Cairo of my youth and a piece of Egyptian history. It was opened at the beginning of 20<sup>th</sup> century and by 1915 was something of a literary cafe. It was also a place where revolutionaries met to hatch plots against various regimes. It is situated in Soliman Pacha Street (now Talaat Harb) near the 'Yacoubian building' of the novel and film, and a stone's throw from the famous Patisserie Groppi. My father used to patronise it and played backgammon there when we lived in nearby Antikhana (now Mahmoud Bassiouni) Street. As I walked passed it, I noticed that it had been lovingly restored but seemed closed. I took a few photographs and noticing a few people inside tried the door. "I am sorry", said a middle-aged man in English. "It is closed". I replied in Arabic that I wanted to take some photographs inside, as my father used to play 'tawla' there 60 years ago. "Welcome, welcome please come in. Will you have a coffee?" Calling the waiter he said "Felfel bring a sada (with no sugar) for the bey". Felfel turned out to be the only remaining waiter and was 83. When told about my father he thought he remembered him. Thinking that he was trying to flatter me, I asked who his adversaries were. He immediately gave me the correct names. I was stunned and moved to tears about this. Felfel is a Nubian who started working at the Cafe Riche in 1943 at the age of 13. He was still battling on and has become something of a media star. A long article about him and the Café Riche has appeared in the Financial Times very recently.

Michel, the owner, showed me round the restored cafe and took me to the basement which had a secret door behind the bar, and which was used by plotters when the police searched the place. It led to a tunnel which opened on to a nearby square. Michel and I continued to chat about the old times of the Riche and about Middle Eastern politics. He told me that he thought that there had been three countries which had been a disaster (mousiba) for the Middle East: the US, Israel and Saudi Arabia. I said that I tended to agree partly, but would add the leaders of the Palestinians, who had been 'homars' (donkeys). If they had played their cards right they could have had a much larger, independent Palestinian state than they were now reduced to try and get. He asked me whether I would still be in Cairo on the next Friday. I was not sure about the time of my return flight but said that I would check. It turned out that they have a literary brunch every Friday at 12noon. I found that it would be possible to check out of my hotel come to the brunch with my suit-cases and get to the Airport in time.

I arrived shortly after noon with my bags and packs of spices for my daughter. Felfel put them aside and I moved into the main dining room where a handful of writers had already assembled. I got into conversation with Magda Mehdawy, a cookery writer who had recently published a book on Ancient Egyptian Cookery, and with her Egyptologist co-author, Amr Hussein, who gave me a copy of his book on Egyptian slang which is in English. I thumbed through the book and congratulated him of filling an important gap in the market for those who were interested in Egypt but did not understand its language. I noted however that some words were missing and pointed this out to him. He asks "Which words are missing?" "Well, for instance, the words for 'fart", I replied. "I think English speakers would be interested to find out that Arabic is one of the only language that has two words (some say three) for this. 'Zarta' for the noisy one and 'Fassia' for the silent, but deadly one". "But it's rude", he said. "All slang includes a high proportion of rude words", I replied. I then noticed that the text had been self- censured and that words, indicating body parts or having a sexual connotation, had all been excluded again on grounds of rudeness. I encouraged him to include such words as 'labua' and 'sharmouta' (whore) as well as body parts, and told him this would add greatly to a second edition and be a great success with foreign visitors. I turned to Magda and found that many of my favourite Egyptian dishes were well-known to the ancient Egyptians and were portrayed on the walls of pharaonic tombs, eg molokheya and foul medames (fava beans), taameya (falafel), chickpea mixtures and, especially, the typical bread of Egypt which like a round mottled pitta but with dark-brown patches. This is generally known as 'gheish baladi'. The only later imports from the Americas were aubergines, potatoes and tomatoes. The start of a conversation on deserts was interrupted by an engineer from Damieta, who intervened to say that many of the deserts thought to be Egyptian were, in fact, French imports from the time of Khedive Ismail.

We sat down to a simple peasant meal of foul medames, taameya, tahina and a vast amount of Gheish Baladi (the greyish pitta like bread of the poor which is slightly gritty because it is said to include some millet in the flour). I put some loaves in my bag as it is one of the few foods not obtainable in London. There were about 40 writers and this marked a return to the Cafe Riche of old. Michel introduced me as someone who was born round the corner in Antikhana Street and whose father used to play tawla in the Cafe Riche 60 years ago. People gathered around me with friendly words of welcome. I was so excited by the goings on that I could hardly remain seated and, with each lull in the conversation, I dashed out to nearby Midan Talaat Harb with its statue of T.H and the famous art deco marvel of Patisserie Groppi, and its two excellent bookshops where I nipped in from time to time to buy books which came up in the conversation. We were served with a desert, which I had not had before, and I made a hasty get-away to Cairo Airport with shouts of "come back" echoing behind me.

The Cafe Riche is a relatively smart place in the centre of modern Cairo. More common throughout the city are the small local places with a few tables invariably patronised by men only who sit around chatting, playing dominoes or backgammon, sipping dark tea in small glasses and perhaps smoking a chicha. The substance smoked is called ma'sal It usually consists of either thickened plain molasses with a bit of tobacco or fruit–based molasses, the most common being apple. They are kept alight with red hot charcoal (fahm) placed delicately on top of the molasses and kept going by the youngest waiter. Self-lighting forms of charcoal are now available for ease of use at home. The best are made from coconut shells.

Finally, there are the larger traditional tea houses of which 'Fishawi' in the Khan el Khalili is the most famous example. It is said to have been patronised by the novelist Naguib Mahfouz. This is laid out with small tables occupying most of a small pedestrianised side-street with an additional large room. I have often stopped for a tea and shisha there and engaged in conversation with tourists from the Lebanon or from other neighbouring countries. The material smoked in a shisha is called 'ma3sal'.It consists largely of molasses from various fruit mixed with a variable amount of tobacco, usually about 10-20%. It is lit with charcoal (fahm). Although at first thought to be less harmful than cigarettes, it is at least as harmful if not more so. Some say that one shisha is equivalent to about 40 cigarettes. It is however less addictive as the nicotine content is low. The pleasure comes from a combination of 'playing' with odoriferous smoke (my favourite is apple), hearing the bubbling through the water and, of course, the whole ritual of lighting it which is usually done by a waiter, who also keeps it going by adding more charcoal when needed. Self-lighting charcoal is now available for home smoking .Fishawi has a great variety of flavours and it is possible to spend the whole day the whole day there chatting and gossiping far from the cares of everyday life and without a Mamnou' to be heard except for alcoholic drinks which were never served. It is to all intents and purposes the typical middle class Egyptian cafe and a great place to relax away from the hectic cauldron which is Cairo.

# Chapter 14

# SHISHA (HOOKAH) AND MAZAG

No one visiting the Middle East, let alone walking along the Edgware Road in London, can fail to be struck by the men puffing away at their shisha. This has never been an exclusively male habit as will be clear from Delacroix's 'Femmes d'Alger' and other Orientalist paintings. This water-pipe variously known as shisha (in the Middle East) hubble-bubble (English Colonial), hukah (in India), narghile(in Turkey) and Qalian (in Iran) has a long and venerable history with an origin in the 16$^{th}$ century.

According to some writers the idea of bubbling tobacco smoke through water in order to purify it is usually attributed to Abd-el-Fath el Gilani ,a Persian physician at the Indian Moghul court of Emperor Jalal-ud-Din Mohamad el Akbar the third Moghul of the dynasty in 1588. However, there is an earlier mention in a rubayat by the Persian poet Ahli el Shirazi.Credit for its invention is therefore lost in the ill-documented Arabo-Indian literature of the 16th century. Its first use probably arose somewhere in Persia or in the Indian sub-continent.

The shisha consists of several elements:

- The bowl that holds the tobacco mixture and charcoal.
- The windscreen which is optional and protects the glowing embers from any prevailing wind.
- The pipe or hose usually consisting of a flexible tube to which is attached.
- The jar containing water or an aromatic fluid such as rose water. The stem leading from the bowl comes down into the water and hangs below it so that the smoke passes down through the water into the hose.
- A purge valve, which is present in some pipes and allows stale smoke to be evacuated if the shisha as not been use for some time.
- The plate which is usually a sort of copper tray surrounding the bowl. It has a double function acting to collect any ash dropping out of the bowl and a shelf on which to place the tweezer, used to pick up hot charcoal, and a small metal rod useful for clearing any blockage in the system.
- Finally, there are a number of sealing grommets to ensure that no leaks occur at the various connections.

The mixture usually smoked consists of molasses which may be fruit flavoured mixed with a variable quantity of tobacco usually amounting to 20%. I like the apple-flavoured molasses produced by the Egptia firm of Nakhla, but some prefer stronger mixtures with no flavour. I also tend to add some rose water into the bowl. The mixture is placed n he bowl and glowing charcoal (called fahm) placed upon it and replenished by a junior waiter in a café. At home, if no barbecue is going, one uses quick-lighting tablets of charcoal first produced for burning incense or small pieces of charcoal made from coconut or other wood. These were set alight by being placed on a lit gas hob.

## Shisha (Hookah) and Mazag

In countries where smoking in-doors is Mamnou', the shisha is smoked outside at a table on pavement .This can be seen in such places as the Edgware Road in London. As most cafes in Cairo are open to the street, smoking in cafe has not altered significantly. However, health concerns have led to the introduction of disposable hoses.

I have smoked shishas in different settings in Cairo. Soon after my arrival I ordered an apple-flavoured one at the Coffee Pot in Abul Feda Street at the foot of the Om Kalthoum Hotel. This was a trendy cafe with many young people with both men and women smoking. The shishas were all designer types with disposable hoses. This was the place where I was accosted by the young woman who wanted to meet Omar Sherif and where I had a big Mamnou' argument with the manager.

More usually, I would go round the corner to a simple intimate cafe with predominantly elderly men smoking and having tea or coffee which was all that was served. There were no female customers and the shishas were very basic with no disposable parts and no choice of flavour.

I often engaged the locals in conversation. All wanted to know where I came from, where I had learned to smoke and whether shishas were smoked in my country. I supplied the information and usually asked what they got from having a shisha. They usually replied that they felt relaxed and peaceful as they heard the smoke bubbling through the water and they experienced 'mazag' (an untranslatable word meaning quiet enjoyment). Few smoked cigarettes as well. When asked how cigarettes and shishas differed, they said that they smoked cigarettes to get energy but they never gave them 'mazag. Did they ever smoke hashish in the shisha? "No that would be a waste as all the hash would go up in the smoke".

The third setting where I had a shisha was at Fishawi's cafe in the Khan el Khalili Market. This was a favourite of Naguib Mahfouz. It is a large traditional establishment astride a lane in the market – a more middle class affair though neither smart nor trendy. There was a choice of flavour, no disposable hose but an optional wind shield. The service is prompt and the waiter replenishes the pipe as and when needed. I sat there and had a relaxed conversation with a Lebanese man who was in Cairo on business.

The pursuit of the shisha turns out to expose the visitor to a good cross- section of Cairo life and opens the way to relaxed conversations.

# Chapter 15

# A PICNIC AT QANATER EL KHAYREYA (THE DAMS OF WELFARE)

One Friday morning, I thought I would go on a picnic to a park next to a dam to the North of the City. When people speak of a dam on the Nile, this usually invokes the High Dam south of Aswan built by Nasser in the 1960s, with Russian funding. To those whose childhood was spent in Cairo the word 'dam' or barrage means something else. Twenty kilometres north of Cairo, where the Rosetta and Damietta branches of the Nile divide up to form the beginning of the Delta, are a series of much smaller dams built in 1863 on the initiative of Mohamed Ali.

This was and remains a favourite picnic spot. Traditionally, the feast of Sham al Nassim, marking the beginning of Spring, was the usual time for taking the two-hour boat trip. This 'fosha' (promenade) was very much on both the King Farouk's and President Sadat's calendar but it has become very much a people's event. I had previously taken it in the 1980s with my friend and ex-neighbour, Freddy Benghiat (now deceased), whose family originated from Aden. We were mobbed by school children who were attracted by my cigarillos and pestered me endlessly for a puff. On this occasion I embarked on the Corniche Maspero opposite the Telecom building. The return ticket cost LE10 (just over £1) for the four to six-hour return boat trip.

The boat was full of Egyptian families, teenagers and students, and the atmosphere was ebullient with much singing, dancing and hand-clapping. The boat went past the inner and outer suburbs of Cairo, past Shubra which reminded me that I had to go there to look for the remnants of my old school. The outward trip took two hours and we were met on arrival by hordes of 'hantours' (horse driven carriages), donkeys, horses and motor-rickshaws and other assorted modes of transport offering to take us on rides to different places. I was among the few who went walking over the three parts of the dam over which ran bridges with numerous men with fishing rods held above the water of the Nile. I asked what they caught and was told it was 'bolti' (tilapia or perch). I made my way towards a somewhat dilapidated village with a couple of deserted restaurants. I stopped at the second and was shown some wriggling tilapia. I asked for one to be grilled for me and it was served simply with some tehina and flat bread as a starter. Although I understand that this fish is widely farmed, I assumed that the one I got was caught by one of those fishing on the bridges. Anyway, although somewhat bland, it was most acceptable.

After this light collation, I made my way back to the pontoon and, on the way, met many of my fellow travellers packing up their picnics. We just made it back to the boat. The return journey was slower, partly because we were going against the current, but also because we picked up another boat which had run out of fuel and was lashed to our own. We took four hours to return. On the way back I saw a sole foreign couple. It turned out that she was an English employee of the WHO (World Health Organisation) and he was a retired American professor of medical history who looked like Mark Twain. He was an expert on

## A picnic at Qanater el Khayreya (the dams of Welfare)

epidemics and was currently engaged in writing about one of the cholera epidemics of the Crimean war. He was very dismissive of Florence Nightingale who was his 'bete noire'. He blamed her for the death of many, because of her antiquated ideas about cholera and about much more.

It looked as though he was preparing a hatchet job on her to finish off where Lytton Strachey had started in 'Eminent Victorians'. They had lived in a very smart part of central Cairo near the British and American Embassies, called 'Garden City' for the past 20 years. I spent the rest of the journey speaking to them and to a young Egyptian couple of newly-weds. We admired some of the impressive large villas which lined the route and were apparently owned by local officials and rich Cairenes.

Altogether a most agreeable and interesting excursion out of Cairo, but not one for the faint–hearted, as the place can be very dirty. I took Aykan, my Turkish girl-friend, now my wife, on the trip but she found the experience disagreeable and the places disgusting. While on the subject of boats, a few words about the others would not be out of place.

## Chapter 16

# FELOUKAS AND DAHABEYAS - FLOATING PALACES AND FLOATING BROTHELS

*T*he Nile has always accommodated many vessels dating from time immemorial. In my mind, they are all associated with sex. By the time I was a teenager, the brothels of Clot Bey Street had long been closed down. Clot Bey was a French physician who brought Western medicine to Egypt. It is a wry fate for his name to be linked with brothels and prostitutes. In my youth, I heard many tales of famous 'horizontales' whom these houses of pleasure gave room to. I remember one who was renowned for eating 'lib' (melon seeds) while her young clients were hushing and puffing on top of her. At a crucial stage, while spitting out a shell, she would say "Khalast ya ebni?" (Have you finished my son?). This reminds me of the first and only time I went to a brothel. I was about 16 and was sitting with friends in Florian's in Venice at the end of a tour of Italy. There had been a naval strike and we were stuck in Venice for an extra week at the expense of 'The Adratica Company' who ran the 'Hesperia' on which we were booked. A beautiful woman passed by and I expressed my admiration very enthusiastically. An older Egyptian sitting nearby sighed rather wearily: "Laboua" (a prostitute). I said it was impossible. "See how pure she looks". "Come with me son", he replied and, after following him through small Venice streets, we arrived at a plush house with a velvet covered 'salon' where men were sitting having coffee and drinks while being entertained by bare-breasted women. I saw her there and went off with her up the stairs. "What shattered illusions!'

The days of those 'horizontales' were now long gone and business had moved to the feluccas (lateen sailing boats seen throughout Egypt which plied their trade along the river). You hailed one, did your business, washed in Nile water and returned to land. It is a wonder that sexually transmitted diseases were not more prevalent in the middle class youth of Cairo. In fact, I never heard of any who contracted one. The boats were perhaps more romantic than their predecessors in the Rue Clot Bey but they, too, became Mamnou' and I don't know where the latest 'knocking shops are now'. Ordinarily, feloukas can, nevertheless, still be hired for quite innocent romantic trips of a few hours. They can be boarded either opposite the Intercontinental Hotel or, more cheaply, near the Ramses Hilton. The Nile in Cairo also accommodates house-boats known as 'dahabeyas'. Many of the larger ones have been turned into expensive but not very good restaurants. At one time, there was a notorious one which was a favourite meeting-place for gay men who have a tough time in Egypt. A couple of years ago it was 'busted' and many people arrested. The gay world has gone underground, but being a heterosexual, I have not penetrated this particular secret and now very 'Mamnou' world.

Dahabeyas can also be hired in Luxor and Aswan for Nile cruises. Agatha Christie's 'Murder on the Nile' features one of these as it does the famous Cataract Hotel in Aswan. They are slower but more romantic than the usual cruise–boats all of which have been badly affected by the current political situation in Egypt which has had a dire effect on tourism More prosaically, there are lines of them moored along the Nile in Cairo, which serve as permanent homes for middle class families or even, second homes, for wealthier people. On one of them, there has been established 'Dr Ragab's Papyrus Museum'. This enterprising man, in his retirement, turned to an interest in the cultivation of the plants, their harvesting and in all the stages in the production of papyrus leaves for the writing of books. He wrote a PhD thesis on the subject of the Museum he created. This is now owned and run by his children who also sell examples of classical papyri and will make one to order. I had one made which is a copy of an ancient one describing the symptoms of dementia or depressive pseudo-dementia in old age. Recently, I had another celebrating my son-in-law's 50th birthday in hieroglyphs. I recommend them as original presents for all occasions.

These house boats were much used during the period known as 'La Belle Époque'. This is an indefinite time which is definitely pre-1952 and extending backwards to the reign of the Khedive Ismail, who greatly admired all things French and commissioned many European-type buildings.

# Chapter 17

# LA BELLE ÉPOQUE

Soon after my arrival on my second trip, I received a call from Nasser who said: "Are you doing anything tonight?" I told him "I have an appointment with my friend Tambal ". Tambal is a man who makes the best 'taameyas' in Zamalek. When not too busy, he allows me to try my hand at chucking the raw mixture into boiling oil. Nasser persuaded me to cancel it as he was proposing an interesting evening in Maadi with dinner at a nearby plush restaurant called 'La Belle Époque'. As Tambal was often closed in the evening, the altered arrangements did not present any problems.

I made my way to Maadi, using the very efficient Metro system and was impressed as usual by the courtesy of the other passengers, one of whom invariably offered me a seat. I was never sure about whether this was because of my age or because I was a foreigner.

Maadi is a smart southern suburb of Cairo, planned under the realm of Khedive Tewfik by three Jewish bankers, who obtained a concession to build in 1888. Although a few kilometres from downtown Cairo, it is relatively easily accessible by public transport or by car along the Nile. It has too, a certain extent, replaced Zamalek as the choice area of the upper middle class and has gradually become increasingly self-contained with its own smart shops and restaurants. It is possible to live for years in Cairo without stepping out of Maadi. Many rich Egyptians and employees of multinationals do so.

Nasser and his wife (now deceased) occupied the top floors of the parental villa. When I arrived I met some of the other guests who consisted of a business man and his wife, a couple employed by a working for a major pharmaceutical company, and a middle-aged lady who worked for a Non-Governmental Organisation (NGO) in Geneva and was in Cairo on one of her occasional yearly visits.

We settled down for drinks and tit-bits. In middle class Egypt, the pre-prandial period is relatively long with a large choice of drinks and the opportunity to drink quite a lot. Little, if any, drink is usually offered during the meal although on this occasion, there was some excellent Chianti and some acceptable South African-inspired local Chardonnay in the dining room of the hotel/restaurant. Things are different in the Loza family.

Conversation hinged on the current state of the Presidency and the role which the then President's wife had come to play in day-to-day affairs of state. The consensus was that Mubarak would probably be followed by his son in 2011.How wrong can you be in forecasting the future in Egypt? Scorn was poured over Nobel Prize winner El Barradei's chances in the absence of a political base. We spoke a lot about the cinema and I told them of my increasing difficulty in putting names to faces in the case of old films, eg I can never remember James Cagney's name though I have no trouble with Humphrey Bogart who is of roughly the same period. Big pharma and his wife showed a surprisingly excellent memory in this regard. I have seldom come across people so adept at remembering names of films, their directors and actors, with mind blowing rapidity.

In Egypt, the term 'La Belle Époque' usually refers to the period of the Fouad and Farouk monarchies and the plush style associated with it. In this case, it was the name of a restaurant.

## La Belle Époque

The 'La Belle Époque' restaurant was indeed plush. Part of a boutique hotel, it was decorated in 'Louis Farouk' (a parody of Louis XV) style. I gather that the bedrooms are very comfortable and in the same style. The food consisted of excellent international bistro cuisine with a smattering of Egyptian food with an imaginative twist. I stuck to my favourite lentil soup and a tagine of fish, Port Said-style. In the absence of the sea bass mentioned on the menu this was an excellent Nile perch. This was followed by a variety of ice creams and sorbets and the ubiquitous but delicious Um Ali. All this inspired me to sing 'Chevaliers de la table Ronde', 'Les Filles de La Rochelle' and other French drinking or bawdy songs accompanied by big pharma's wife who had been brought up in French-speaking Lebanon.

The evening was very much a throw back to 'La Belle Époque'

I got a lift back to my hotel from the NGO lady from Geneva in her hired car.

# Chapter 18

# A ROTARY CLUB BREAKFAST

*I* always enjoy meeting writers and journalists when I am in Cairo. On one occasion last year, I was buying books in the excellent 'Diwan' bookshop when I was told that Alaa el Aswany, the author of The Yacoubian Building would be giving a talk followed by a 'Question and answer' session to launch his latest book of essays on 'The State of Egypt'. Al Aswany who is a dentist has been very active in the recent political turmoil in Egypt and has been a strong supporter of El Baradei for president. Knowing of this interest of mine, my friend, Talaat Badrawi, rang me. "The novelist, Samia Serageldin, a cousin of mine, is giving a talk at the Marriott tomorrow. Are you interested?" "Sure, that is just the thing I am here for." Samia is an Egyptian writer currently living in the US. She has written an interesting semi- autobiographical novel called 'The Cairo House', which exposes the ups and downs of a wealthy and prominent Egyptian family from the 1950s until today. As most of the accounts I have read have concerned Jewish families or conversations with poorer people, I thought this would prove a good contrast. The attraction of the talk added to the fact that it was taking place in my favourite Cairo hotel, The Marriott, built for the visit of Empress Eugenie, making it irresistible for me.

The talk was part of a series of breakfast meetings of one of the Rotary Club chapters of Cairo. I am told of the principal principle Rotary Clubs, one has mainly German-educated members and the other mainly English-educated ones. Although this was the mainly 'German one' I heard only English and Arabic being spoken. As I had not brought a suit with me, I wore an orange sports jacket but was, nevertheless, welcomed by the assembled company. In her blog written after the meeting, Samia wickedly described me as wearing an orange track-suit.

The Serageldin and Fakhr el Islam and Badrawi families to which Samia belongs are representatives of the important landowning Muslim families who were founding members of the Wakf party under the old regime. They provided many of the ministers who ruled the country but, at the same time, exercised a steady 'anti-colonial' policy aimed at getting rid of Britain's 'protection'. After writing the 'Cairo House', Samia went on to her second novel 'The Naqib's Daughter', which is set during the Napoleonic invasion and is remarkably accurate in its background history. In her talk, she tried to draw parallels between the Anglo-American invasion of Iraq and that of Napoleon in Egypt. This parallel was questioned by the audience who found the comparison somewhat strained. In particular, the Napoleonic invasion - despite its doubtful motives - did include an important academic component which led to the development of Egyptology and other related sciences. Although it is often portrayed as a generally benign affair, it was in fact punctuated by fierce opposition and repression well described by el Jabarty. The discussion was nevertheless lively and interesting.

As I was feeling hungry, I made my way to Abu Tarek in Champollion Street, rumoured to have the best 'Koshary' in Cairo. This mixture of small macaronis, rice, lentils topped with fried onions and a strong dose of hot chillies, is now the most popular and cheapest street food. I did not know it when I lived in Cairo as it was, essentially, 'village' food and only became prominent when the village invaded the city well after

## A Rotary Club Breakfast

our departure. Abu Tarek is a large restaurant spread over two floors and decorated with large mirrors and photos of the owner. The ground floor is reserved for take-away and rapid service, the second floor for family meals.

I went to the second floor, was seated at a window table and offered a menu. A variety of local dishes are served but the most popular are the Abu Tarek Koshary and the Special, with extra lentils and onions. Additional chillies were available for those who preferred it spicier.

I took the ordinary one and tucked in to an excellent plate of food sold for a pittance. The service was excellent and I had the company of a Malaysian family at the next table, as the restaurant has now become part of the knowledgeable tourist drag, though the majority of clients remain locals. This was, incidentally, Christmas Day. While sitting there, I was thinking about how agreeable Cairo life could be for the reasonably well–off and how intolerable for the poor and dispossessed. How and why did they put up with it? Why were there no riots or revolutions? When I discussed this with Egyptian friends they all believed that no revolution would occur as the people had always tolerated authoritarian regimes from the time of the pharaohs. This was barely a month before the Tahrir Square events which got rid of President Mubararak and his circle, and so transformed political life in Egypt.

# Chapter 19

# IBN TULUN MOSQUE, THE GAIR ANDERSON MUSEUM AND THE ISLAMIC MUSEUM

On Boxing Day, I thought I should return to visit some Muslim Monuments. In his excellent guide to Egypt, my friend, Michael Haag, says: "If you have time to visit only one Islamic monument, the mosque of Ibn Tulun should be your choice". I could not agree more and seldom pass through Cairo without at least a short visit. If one were to extend Michael Haag's choice further I would add the Sultan Hassan Mosque and, for the brave, the Mausoleums of the City of the Dead, particularly those of Qait Bey and Barquq. The driver of the taxi I hailed, though Cairo born, did not know where it was and had to be directed there. I was somewhat surprised by this though I understand that it is not unusual. He also lacked the usual jaunty Cairo wisdom of many of his colleagues roaming the city but, finally, dropped me outside the mosque though seemed at a loss about how to get back wherever he was going.

Built in 876-879 by Governor Ibn Tulun, the Mosque immediately betrays its Mesopotamian and Abbassid origins. Its minaret with its helical structure is one of the most unusual I have seen. The ziyadah (courtyard) of the mosque is one of the most peaceful places in Cairo, as apart from the very rare tourist bus, it is seldom visited. It lies somewhat outside the main concentration of Islamic monuments but well within sight of the Citadel which attracts so many more tourists. I spent a while relaxing in this architectural gem and chatting to the attendants who collected the shoes of those who came to pray or to visit. A lucrative, if sometimes smelly, existence. Shoes are, of course, Mamnou'.

On my way out of the Mosque, I felt that, since I was in the area, I might as well remind myself of the Gayer-Anderson House whose entrance is nearby. Otherwise known as Beit el Kitlleya (House of the Cretan Woman) it consists of two houses which have been knocked into one. It is a real warren, much of it 17th century with Musharabeya wood-work. I usually turn my nose at it as containing a lot of 'knick-knacks'. So it does, but I found it is more attractive than I remembered. The house used to belong to a doctor in the British army and each room is decorated in a particular ethnic style. As I wanted to have it to myself, I lied to the numerous, all too helpful attendants and told them , that - as the doctor was my ancestor - I knew the house well and did not require any help in seeing it. I think that they only half-believed me but did leave me alone. I was not attacked as James Bond was in 'The Spy Who Loved Me' filmed in this house.

Not far from these buildings lies the Islamic Museum. It previously held an impressive collection which was poorly displayed. The Museum had been closed for several years for restoration and it was only toward the end of 2010 that I was able to revisit it. It is now a gem beautifully reorganised by a French designer. The displays are shown chronologically on one side and thematically on the other. It is a real treat.

After this feast of Islamic architecture, I felt the need to see something more Western in its evocations. The Opera seemed just the thing.

## Chapter 20

# THE OPERA HOUSE AND MUSEUM OF MODERN ART

The Cairo Opera House evokes all sorts of memories for me. The original, built to commemorate the opening of the Suez Canal, was supposed to be inaugurated with Verdi's 'Aida' with a libretto by Mariette Pacha, the French Egyptologist. In the event, the opera was not ready in time and the opening featured 'Rigoletto'. Situated in the Ezbekeya Gardens, opposite the old Shepheard's Hotel, it played an important part of Cairo cultural life and was, in addition, the main theatre used in visits by the Comedie Francaise and The Old Vic Company. I remember seeing Louis Jouvet in 'Knock' and 'Le Malade Imaginaire', and 'The Rivals' as well as being initiated to opera with 'Aida'.

The original building was destroyed by a fire 1971 and the replacement, which is now situated on the island of Gezira behind the statue of Saad Zaghloul, was built with Japanese finance and a Japanese architect, Koichiro Chikida, in 1988. It is an attractive, relatively plain building with oriental arches and a pointed dome. The exterior has a distinct Islamic feel about it and the interior has a mixture of Eastern and Western influences, with occasional Pharaonic reminders. It occupies a large park, which also houses a smaller hall and the Museum of Modern Art.

I booked seats for a performance of 'Blood Wedding' - a flamenco ballet, inspired by the Frederico Garcia Lorca text, and performed by the Antonio Gaudi company. I was informed that ties were compulsory. The audience was dressed 'to the nines' with many mink coats to be seen. There was a striking absence of hejabs - in contrast with the 80% covered women's heads seen in the street.

The Museum of Contemporary Art is in the grounds of the Opera complex. It has a number of attractive paintings by Egyptian artists mostly modern, rather than truly contemporary. I found it disappointing considering the talented modern Arabic & Islamic Art I have seen in London. Notably absent are works using Arabic calligraphy as a starting point. There is was no catalogue available in any language and the multilingual DVD does not work.

Across the road from the Opera Complex is the small but intriguing Mokhtar Museum.

Mahmoud Mokhtar was an Egyptian sculptor of the early 20$^{th}$ century who made something of a specialty of the building of statues. Those most well-known are the Saad Zaghloul statue on the island of Gezira and the Awakening of Egypt, now just outside Cairo University and the Zoo. The Museum exhibits many of his smaller works and points to his success in Paris in the 1920s. For his larger works, one needs to explore the streets of Cairo for the wonderful statues he built. That of the early revolutionary Saad Zaghloul always makes my spine tingle and brings back many memories of playing and learning in Cairo. Photography is Mamnou' in the Museum which seems a pity as there is no danger to the works from flash lighting and no reproductions are available. I smuggled my camera in and though I was far from any attendant, the first picture I took made one pop out of nowhere shouting "Mamnou'".

# Chapter 21

# WAITING FOR OMAR

*I* have earlier outlined the trajectory of my schooling from the French Cours Morin to the English Gezira Preparatory School and, eventually, to Victoria College. I regret that I have been unable completely to retrace my steps there physically with the exception of my last school in Maadi. Gezira Preparatory school no longer exists except as the remnants of a gate near the Anglican Cathedral in Zamalek. The Old Victoria College Cairo which was, during World War II, located in a confiscated Italian school in the popular and predominantly Coptic borough of Shubra, was

I later transferred to the smart suburb of Maadi. I was unable to find the Shubra building but had no difficulty in locating the Maadi one where I spent my last two years in the new building which still exists as the renamed 'Victory College'. (Fig 14) Two very different famous individuals have either written or spoken about their own schooling which overlapped with my own - Omar Sharif and the late Edward Said. In this process of reminiscence, I have tried to establish contacts with them. Alas, in the case of Edward this was limited to an exchange of letters following the appearance of his auto biographical 'Out of Place'. In that of Omar Sharif, bad luck seems to have kept us apart with the exception of one telephone call from London to his room in the Intercontinental Hotel.

Victoria College was a pale imitation of an English Public School. The teaching was generally indifferent but there was a handful of inspiring teachers. For Chemistry, I will always remember Zaki Iskandar, who was a great inspiration and, for French, there was the charismatic Raoul Parme who was an expert on Petrarch and clearly homosexual in inclination. Zaki Iskandar later became a medical historian and I saw him again in London where he was working for the Wellcome History Library.of Raoul Parme. I know only that he ended his life in Cairo as greatly impoverished. He sold poems to the parents of ex-Victoria College pupils. There was also a motley array of other teachers I remember. The Headmaster, Mr Price, who suffered from piles and sat on an inflatable rubber ring; a gay teacher who was stabbed by a homosexual lover and left Egypt under a cloud after the affair was hushed up; and, a Mr Dodds, who found himself with a penis in his hand when he searched all the pupils' pockets, after he heard a gunshot in the class. The boy concerned had made a hole in pocket. We were a pretty delinquent lot.

We played no rugby as the ground was too hard, so it was football in winter and cricket in summer. I was poor at both. As a full back, I was neither fast nor tough enough to act as an effective defender and the subtleties of cricket were lost on me I tried to avoid games as often as possible on the grounds that my sports were tennis (the school had no courts) and swimming (no pool either). Omar Sharif, or Michel Chalhoub as I knew him then, was good at both football and cricket as was my classmate the late Loic Hemsy, who was 'left wing'. As far as Omar is concerned, I must blame his technophobia and complicated life for having lost anything but telephonic contact, but have not yet given up the dinner that we were to have together in Cairo last March. He and I overlapped at Victoria College and, although he was a year ahead of me, we were in the same class for French under the late Raoul Parme. Monsieur Parme, as we knew him, was a French- speaking Maltese who frightened most boys because of his fiercely critical approach to education. He was known then as a poet and translator of Petrarch and his tenderness towards Omar, on whom he had a crush, was striking. Anyone who got in the way of his admiring glance would be told "Hotes-toi de mon soleil" ("Do not block my sunshine"). One of Parme's artistic activities involved producing classical French plays and it was, as result of this, that Omar (who was already an immensely talented actor) and I found ourselves in 'Le Malade Imaginaire' - he as the son of Argan the hypochondriac and me, his Docteur Diafoirus. I still have a photograph of a scene from the play (Fig 15) as I also have some of him as part of his house and school football team. It was then his ambition to go to the Royal Academy of Dramatic Art (RADA) in London, but his father, who was a Lebanese timber merchant, put his foot down. Of course, there was no stopping him and, partly as a result of being discovered by film director Youssef Chahine, he found his way into Egyptian films assisted partly by his marriage to Fatem Hamama, the film star. For some time after we both left school, our paths would cross notably in London in the 1970s when he was participating in a bridge tournament at the old Europa Hotel in Grosvenor Square. On that occasion, he made a pass at my then wife asking her if I satisfied her in bed. We subsequently lost touch and I realised recently that we probably had not met for 40 years. Following the showing of the film 'Al Musafer' (The Traveller) at the London Film Festival which I greatly enjoyed, I was determined to tell him how good I thought the film was. I got in touch with his secretary in Paris (who told me he hated the film) and found that during my next trip to Cairo, I was going to miss him again as he was due in Qatar on the day of my arrival. However, she gave me his room number at the Semiramis Intercontinental in Cairo (he does not do email). I rang the hotel and was put through to him. We had a brief chat during which he insisted that his secretary was mistaken and that he would in fact be in Cairo during my next visit and suggested dinner together. We arranged to ring one another, but there was only his Voicemail when I tried, eventually, and it became clear that, either he was avoiding me or was in Qatar as his Paris secretary predicted. Was it all what is called a boat man's invitation (Ghuzumat al Marakbeya)? - the term used for a hollow invitation since it is issued by the boat man on his Felouka in the middle of the Nile to someone on the river bank.

Although I did not realise it at the time, Edward Said's education overlapped even more closely with mine and some of his school experiences were uncannily close to mine. When I was Gezira Preparatory School, I once got into trouble with the Headmaster, Mr Keith Bullen, when I wrote 'I love Mary Kate' in a prayer book. (We were then all in love with Mary Kate Miles). This was a serious Mamnou' act. As a result I received a caning - 'six of the best'. For years I kept the memory of a red-faced bully who would have been more suited to run a concentration camp than act as a headmaster of a Cairo school. Imagine my surprise when reading 'Cairo in the War' by Artemis Cooper, many years later, to discover that Bullen was an aesthete, a poet, a friend of Laurence Durrell and editor of one of the only English poetry magazine published in Egypt. On reading Edward's 'Out of Place', I found him describing a similar episode where he was given the cane and imagined Bullen as a brutal representative of British Colonialism, only to be as surprised as I was by Artemis Cooper's revelations. I wrote to him to share his surprise and also to correct another false memory which appeared in his 'Out of Place', where he misnamed my cousin, Maryse Amiel, as Colette and gave her a part as the Queen of Hearts in 'Alice in Wonderland', when she told me that she had, in fact, been in the play but as the Dodo, not the Red Queen. We never had a chance to exchange memories as he died soon after.

While at Gezira Prep, I joined the local Wolf Cubs who used to meet in the Gezira Sporting Club every week. There, I learnt to tie knots, pitch a tent and do other 'scoutish' things as well as intoning the '"Akila we'll do our best." ....promise Our chauffeur, Abdu, who would wait outside and look through the bars was intrigued and enormously amused by the "Did,dib,dob'......" part, which he would repeat to tease me about it from time-to-time.

I never joined the Scouts as such, but in my teens found myself in a small organisation called 'The Young Pioneers'. I later realised that the man leading it was George Blake, the famous KGB agent, who was then George Behar, a Sephardi Jew of Dutch origin. We used to meet on the roof of a building where we planned to publish a comic book. We also discussed agriculture, methods of irrigation and the life of the 'fellahin'. There were bad floods at the time and I was to photograph the plight of the poor for a magazine. This never happened. Although the meetings petered out after a time, it is now clear to me now that though they were not overtly political, Blake had the intention of steering them in that direction and turn us into little communists. He did not succeed, but I sometimes wonder whether he did, perhaps, sow the seeds of my life-long left-wing political orientation.

One final search for a figure of my past - an Egyptian psychiatrist called Ali el Bahtimy, who was at the Maudsley in the 1970s and was responsible for helping me to visit our old flat the first time I returned to Egypt in the early 1980s. By the most amazing coincidence, when my parents were expelled from Egypt during the Suez crisis and their flat was sequestrated, it was his uncle, then an officer in the Egyptian Army, who took over the flat which is still occupied by his cousin. I had been looking for Dr Bahtimy for years and finally, on a recent visit, when I took my daughter and son-in-law to see the flat on waking the occupants in the process, I found that the tenant was Bahtimy's cousin. He gave me his telephone number and address. As his flat was round the corner from his cousin's, I called round and had to wake him up too although it was 10.30am. He seemed delighted to see me and said he had been looking for me for years. We briefly exchanged Maudsley memories and, as I had an appointment elsewhere, I left after exchanging telephone numbers with him. We were to meet for dinner but numerous attempts to reach him failed, even when I rang in the middle of his afternoon siesta and asked his new wife to wake him up, she refused to do. Another mystery.

When doing my hunting down, I usually hail a taxi and the ride almost invariably turns out to be fun.

# Chapter 22

# TAXIS AS A SOURCE OF WISDOM

Every large city has its characteristic taxi-drivers though globalisation has tended to erode the differences. New York, London and Paris taxi drivers are no longer what they were. In Cairo, the differences remain and are highlighted in Khaled al Khamisi witty 'Taxi' which is made up almost entirely by conversations with and anecdotes from local cabbies. This refers largely to the ubiquitous blue and white cabs which, though they have meters, do not use them so that the fare has to be established by prior bargaining in the course of which tourists are 'ripped off'. A typical exchange would be that when asked the price the driver says "Anything you like". Only a firm insistence on a price will achieve a result. Also, not all drivers necessarily know the way to what seems to a tourist to be famous place, eg my driver did not know the way to Ibn Tulun Mosque. Much of the problem arises from the poverty of the public transport other than the excellent Metro and the vast number of cabs (80,000 in 2006), which resulted from President Sadat's decision to allow practically anyone to run a taxi, irrespective of the state of the car or knowledge of the driver.

He passed a further decree facilitating bank loans for taxis. Al Khamisi claims that running a taxi is a not an economic proposition. It is my habit to attempt conversation with the drivers in the course of which I come across both jokey and grumpy types. On arrival in Cairo, after a long flight, I have tended to go for the official fixed price limousines to avoid tiresome bargaining. They are safe, comfortable but dull. Once settled, I then invariably go for the blue and white clapped out cars.

On one journey with my daughter and son-in-law, we found the official limousine office shut and were thrown immediately on to the market. One driver assured us that he had a limousine but wanted LE90 when I knew that he official price was LE70. He refused my offer of LE70 but a competitor said he would take us for LE70 in his 'limousine'. I was not surprised to find that the car was far from being a limousine. He piled our luggage on his roof as his boot failed to open. The car had no seat belts. One of the doors did not close and the man clearly had no idea about the address of our hotel. The car was definitely in a Mamnou' state but no one stopped us. Having guided him there, I found that he overshot his turning and got on to a one way fly-over. "No problem", he said, while he proceeded to drive backwards again a dense traffic. Having arrived at our destination he tried to get an additional amount because of the stress that he had been exposed to a good example of Cairo chutzpah!

Two other cab stories bear recounting. My son-in-law, Ayhan, who was born in Cairo but speaks no Arabic, wished to see the Giza pyramids again. His cousin, Tati, said he need not take a taxi as she would send round her chauffeur to our hotel. Ayhan asked me if I wanted to go with them. "OK, I will come with you but have no particular wish to see the pyramids for the nth time. Just drop me at the Mena House pool and collect me on your way back". We waited in the hotel lobby till Ayhan came in and said "Tati's driver has arrived". We piled into the car and I sat next to the chauffeur and asked for his name "Saad", he said. As soon as we were on the road I asked "How long have you worked for Sit

## Taxis as a source of wisdom

Tati?" "For 40 years", he said. When I passed this information on to Ayhan, he thought it strange as Tati was about 50. "She is only 50", I told the driver. '"Well", he replied "'I worked for the family". "He must have known my father then", exclaimed Ayhan. "Did you know Zakaria Bey?" "Yes, of course". He is in Mecca at the moment. "He is not in Mecca 'I replied. "He is dead and buried". That did not seem to faze him so I assumed that was he a bit muddled because of his advanced age. He dropped me at the Mena House Hotel pool and they went on to their visit of the Pyramids. Less than five minutes later they were back. "Did you not like the Pyramids?" "No, Tati is on my mobile asking where we are as her chauffeur, Sherif, was still waiting for us at our hotel". Realising that we had been conned by a driver claiming to be Tati's driver, I felt like having a row with him and accusing him of being a liar and a thief. However, Tati said she would send Sherif to sort it out. When Sherif arrived, he explained to the guy that he had come to collect us. The driver said "But they have come with me. I want LE100". "That's fine", said Sherif. "Go to this address and ask for Yehia Bey (Ayhan's uncle). He will pay you whatever you want." Of course, he never went to see Yehia but was outside our hotel next morning asking for his money. "Did you go to that address?" "No", he replied. "I was too shy". "Go," I said, "and you will get your money". When my daughter, Simone, came out of the hotel, he was still there asking whether she wanted a taxi! "Not on your life!" she exclaimed.

The other amusing taxi episode occurred on our way back from Ben Ezra Synagogue after an excellent street food lunch of Taameya sandwiches. We walked to the Nile, hoping to take the boat back to town only to find that it was not working, so we stopped a passing cab. My usual opening gambit with taxi drivers is to ask which football team they support. This one replied "I am not interested in football". "Are you interested in any other games?" "Only in bed games", he replied. "But my wife is now 73, so I don't play many games now". When he realised that Simone sitting in the back was my daughter, he apologised profusely for using rude language. I reassured him and told him she did not understand Arabic I moved on to politics. "What do you think of Mubarak?" "I love him". "What about his son?" "I love him too. I love all people in power". "What about El Baradei?" "If he wins the elections, I will love him too!"

Taxi drivers may need to help to get you to the Citadel but are a source of fun if you speak some Arabic. Those who do not should stick to the newer white or grey taxis which are metered or find out ahead of time what a reasonable price for a particular fare is.

A lasting memory I have of my taxi journeys is of being stuck in a vast traffic jam caused by the visit of foreign dignitary. I urged my driver to find a way round but we were stopped by an angry policeman shouting "Mamnou', Mamnou'….. "

# Chapter 23

# AN ALEXANDRIAN INTERLUDE

During my days in Egypt, Cairo was considered to be too hot for the Government to be able to tolerate the high temperature. The King, the Government and all official business were transferred to cooler Alexandria. My family followed and we invariably spent the summer months at the 'Beau Rivage Hotel' and went to Sidi Bishr Number 3 Beach where we had a small 'cabina' (beach house) in Alexandria, which therefore, became an extension of Cairo life. Thus although it was, strictly speaking beyond the remit of this book, I decided to include a chapter on my return there after the recent Tahrir Square events.

I had spent a day there in 1981 but had otherwise not visited the city since my youth. As I had an opportunity of doing so during my last trip to Cairo. I tagged along with Michael Haag and his wife, Lutfeya, (nee Hassanein) who were spending a few days there as Michael had been invited to participate in a 'Round Table', entitled 'Liquid Continents' at the Bibliotheca Alexandrina.

Michael had been promised a car to take us from Cairo to Alexandria. At the last moment, this was not available as he was told that our safety on the desert road could not be guaranteed. My Egyptian friends told me that this was nonsense and, in the event, this Mamnou' 'turned out to be unduly cautious. However, we did take the train which was fast and comfortable, with few stops in the Nile valley, which seemed to have hardly changed from where I was sitting. There were numerous pigeon-coops which had been part of the landscape since Pharaonic times. Pigeons, often stuffed with 'ferik' (broken up wheat) grilled on a spit or oven-roasted remain an important part of the middle class Egyptian menu. The trip was uneventful and, after some haggling with a porter, we took a taxi to the Cecil Hotel where we would be staying.

The Cecil had been the smartest hotel in Alexandria during the Belle Epoque period but had become somewhat faded until it was recently restored to its previous grandeur. I was told by a Muslim acquaintance that it was a hive of Muslim fundamentalism and that he hated staying there, as he felt he was constantly observed in case he indulged in any Mamnou' activities, such as having a glass of beer. To me, there was little sign of this hard-line supervision but I suppose that it is eased for foreign tourists. The service was impeccable and the breakfast buffet splendid. The hotel is currently managed by the French Accor chain, which runs Sofitels and Novotels throughout the world.

I spent the first morning visiting the Eliahu ha Navi (Nabi Daniel) Synagogue and its surrounds in Nabi Daniel Street. I had always been puzzled that a street in Egypt should carry the name of a synagogue, only to find out that the name derives from that of the mosque at the end of the street. The entrance from a side street is well secured but unobtrusive. The Synagogue and the property of the small Jewish community is looked after by Ben Gaon, who is the son of a Cairo tailor who was rumoured to make Presidents Nasser's and Sadat's suits. He was trained in hotel management but hardly practised in this field, though his uncle owns one of the Hilton Hotels in Switzerland. I was ushered

## An Alexandrian interlude

into his office by a Nubian called Abd el Nabi who told me he had worked for the Jewish community for 25 years. Gaon was discussing business with the community lawyer when I arrived. His large office was decorated with old Alexandria pictures and there was a bust of the Baron Jacques de Menasce, founder of the synagogue in 1885, near his desk.

While Gaon was busy, I was shown round the Synagogue by a heavily covered young Nubian woman who was very knowledgeable, spoke good English and had impressive computer skills. She also took me into the garden to see the adjoining Menasce School which is currently leased out to the local government. On my return to Gaon's office, we chatted about the situation and future of the community.

On leaving, I repaired for a foul and falafel (term is used in Alexandria) restaurant at Mohamed Ahmed, currently thought to be one of the best in Alexandria. The owner had bought it from the famous Benyamin, a Jew who had previously owned it till his emigration to the US.

I then made my way to the impressive Bibliotheca Alexandrina to listen to the symposium on 'Liquid Continents'.

This was part of the Library's attempt to develop a higher profile amongst the population, by sponsoring a number of non-bibliographic activities. In this case, it was largely an exploration of the links between Venice, Istanbul and Alexandria. It was mainly attended by professional 'Mediterraneans' who seem to meet in different parts of the world. With a few exceptions, the discussion was somewhat 'airy fairy' with a strong emphasis on Alexandria's Mediterranean past which was hardly necessary. The fact that Istanbul was not a Mediterranean city, neither geographically nor culturally, did not seem to bother the participants.

This was followed by a photographic and painting exhibition which gave me the opportunity of meeting many interesting people, notably the Alexandrian novelist, Ibrahim Abdel Meguid, author of 'No One Sleeps in Alexandria', a couple of brave young painters who had ignored instructions from their College not to participate because of a boycott, and also members of the Polish archaeological team digging at Kom el Dik.

We had dinner at the well-situated Greek Club in the Eastern Harbour. There were no Greeks present but there remain many signs of their past prominence. The famous cafes and the old Patisseries Athineos and Pastroutis remain, though the latter had just closed. The ever-present influence of the poet, Cavafis, whose house has been turned into a museum and the occasional, and surprising, use of Greek words even in modest local cafes, eg when ordering a 'saada' (no sugar) Turkish coffee -I heard the order as 'Wahed skiathos' – a hybrid since 'wahed' means one in Egyptian Arabic and 'skiathos' is the Greek word for 'coffee without sugar'..

On my final day in Alexandria, I chose to look at parts of the City I had never known. I was driven around by Reda, a one-legged and extremely knowledgeable taxi driver. He took me to Montazah where the Royal Palace and grounds were situated. In my time, it was impossible to go much further east than Sidi Bishr beach as the rest was 'Mamnou'' as it was part on the royal Montazah Palace. It was now open to the public and peppered with luxury hotels. As my visit took place just after the Tahrir events, there were numerous tanks stationed in the grounds mostly manned by simple soldiers. Nothing seemed to be Mamnou' - and one of the soldiers offered to give me ride on his tank.

Following this, I was taken to the main Victoria College (now Victory College) which I had never seen before, though I attended the Cairo branch of the school. I took numerous photos of the school but an attempt to visit the school building was declared Mamnou''

I spent the morning before my return to Cairo wandering the streets of Durrell's and Cavafi's Alexandria with Michael Haag, who is currently writing a new biography of Durrell and who, once took Eve Durrell (Lawrence's second wife and part model for Justine), to explore places of her past. Cavafi's flat has been turned into a museum and the street where it is situated had just been named after him.

All in all, I was most impressed by Alexandria which looked much improved as a city in spite of the mad traffic on the Corniche and elsewhere. I was surprised to hear that, in spite of its cosmopolitan past, it had become a stronghold of Islamic fundamentalism.

# Chapter 24

# CONCLUSION

Cairo is known in the Middle-East for the humour of its citizens .The nokta (joke) is generally a favourite form of communication. After last year's referendum on the constitution, I ask a man on the metro who was going to win. "The Orange Party", he exclaimed. Puzzled about the spread of the activities of the telephone company I asked for clarification. I was told that the best way to erase the supposedly indelible ink which marked the finger of those who had voted was to rub it with orange peel. In the latest Presidential election, a wag who was asked whether he had voted, held up his middle finger in a lascivious way. Other favourite nokat (plural of nokta) are stories about Artin, the Armenian; Goha the universal Mediterranean village idiot who is simple but wise; and the Saidi ( man from the South) who is traditionally swindled or shows signs of amazing stupidity and stubbornness. Visitors to Cairo in recent years have been struck by the fact that its inhabitants have, one hopes, temporarily become more reticent, more reserved and much less apt to joke.

In this book, I have tried to give a flavour of what Cairo is like today mainly through conversations and observations in and around some famous places and some not so famous. I have been guided in my choice largely by people and places of which I had clear memories from the Cairo of my youth. Inclusions and exclusions may well appear idiosyncratic but they were dictated, at least partly, by opportunity, familiarity and access. I would have liked to write more about the schools I went to - the Cours Morin, Gezira Preparatory School and Victoria College Shubra and Maadi - but with the possible exception of the last, there is now little trace of these places of learning and fun.

Visitors generally rush through Cairo on their way to Luxor and Aswan. Cairo is certainly not an easy place to get to know but its layers of history and particularly the friendliness and good humour of its citizens repay much greater attention but, then, I am biased as I love the city and think that it well deserves the sobriquet of 'Um el Dunia' (Mother of the World).

Since writing this text much has happened in Egypt and in particular the various manifestations of 'The Arab Spring' which led to the Tahrir Square events which led to the resignation of President Mubarak. The situation is a fluid one and it is difficult to predict what will happen. The Parliamentary elections were held in January 2012. They proceeded quietly and without obvious fraud. The participation rate was 60% and the Muslim Brothers swept to victory with 40%of the vote followed by the Noor party (Salafis with more extreme views) obtaining a surprising 25%. The lay parties which emerged out of the 'Spring Revolution' failed to unite and obtained only a small minority of the votes and seats. The Parliament has now been dissolved by the Army so the significance of these results will remain in doubt.

In the meantime there is chaos in many parts of the country and concerted attacks have been directed at those, whatever their views or area of responsibility, who were appointed during the Mubarak period. A case in point is the way the Director of the Bibliotheca Alexandrina has been treated. The library was besieged and attempts made to set it alight and Mr Serageldine, the Director, threatened with physical violence. Paradoxically,

## Conclusion

the attacks have come not from Islamists but from supposedly progressive and democratic people who share his views.

Recent events in the newly elected parliament when one of the Salafi members shouted "Allah u Akbar" calling others to prayer was called to order by the Muslim Brother Chair and told to leave and go and pray in a nearby Mosque suggests the Brothers may increasingly behave like 'normal' politicians. We are likely to see shifting and increasingly unusua

The latest events have seen the victory of Mohamed Morsi, the Muslim Brother candidate in the Presidential election. This may however prove a hollow victory since the Supreme Army Council has intervened to abolish the Assembly and to take upon itself the power of controlling the budget, directing defence and foreign policy, and choosing who would write the new constitution.

Time will show what kind of regime emerges when the dust has settled. In the meantime, paradox reigns supreme but the spirit of the city of Cairo will surely prevail under the surface.

(END)

Made in the USA
Charleston, SC
11 October 2012